Using Shakespeare's Plays to Explore Education Poli

C000089492

'*Using Shakespeare's Plays to Explore Education Policy Today* is a lucid, well–informed and compelling account of the philosophical basis for market–based social policy in the field of education. In a bold challenge to contemporary orthodoxies in contemporary, market based political economy, Sophie Ward uses strong readings of Shakespeare's plays to discover the deep contradictions in this philosophy in order to reveal its dehumanizing effect on both students and teachers. Dr. Ward's book will be indispensable for anyone concerned with the current state of educational policy, a readership that includes everyone now engaged with teaching and research on Shakespeare.'

Michael D. Bristol, Professor Emeritus, Department of English, McGill University, Canada

Shakespeare is revered as the greatest writer in the English language, yet education reform in the English-speaking world is informed primarily by the 'market order', rather than the kind of humanism we might associate with Shakespeare. By considering Shakespeare's dramatisation of the principles that inform neoliberalism, this book makes an important contribution to the debate on the moral failure of the market mechanism in schools and higher education systems that have adopted neoliberal policy.

The utility of Shakespeare's plays as a means to explore our present socio-economic system has long been acknowledged. As a Renaissance playwright located at the junction between feudalism and capitalism, Shakespeare was uniquely positioned to reflect upon the nascent market order. As a result, this book utilises six of his plays to assess the impact of neoliberalism on education. Drawing from examples of education policy from the UK and North America, it demonstrates that the alleged innovation of the market order is premised upon ideas that are rejected by Shakespeare, and it advocates Shakespeare's humanism as a corrective to the failings of neoliberal education policy.

Using Shakespeare's Plays to Explore Education Policy Today will be of key interest to researchers, academics and students in the fields of education policy and politics, educational reform, social and economic theory, English literature and Shakespeare.

Sophie Ward is Lecturer in the School of Education, Durham University, UK. She is a member of the UK team within the European Policy Network on School Leadership (EPNoSL), a partner-run consortium created in 2011 in response to the increasing European focus on school leaders' professional development, including the preparation and selection of school leaders.

Routledge Research in Education Policy and Politics

For a full list of titles in this series, please visit www.routledge.com

The Routledge Research in Education Policy and Politics series aims to enhance our understanding of key challenges and facilitate on-going academic debate within the influential and growing field of Education Policy and Politics.

Books in the series include

Political and Social Influences on the Education of Children
Research from Bosnia to Herzegovina
Gwyneth Owen-Jackson

The Strong State and Curriculum Reform
Assessing the Politics and Possibilities of Educational Change in Asia
Leonel Lim and Michael W. Apple

Modernising School Governance
Corporate planning and expert handling in state education
Andrew Wilkins

UNESCO without Borders
Educational campaigns for international understanding
Edited by Aigul Kulnazarova and Christian Ydesen

Education and Political Subjectivities in Neoliberal Times and Places
Emergences of norms and possibilities
Edited by Eva Reimers and Lena Martinsson

Local Citizenship in the Global Arena
Educating for community participation and change
Sally Findlow

Using Shakespeare's Plays to Explore Education Policy Today
Neoliberalism through the lens of Renaissance humanism
Sophie Ward

Using Shakespeare's Plays to Explore Education Policy Today

Neoliberalism through the lens of Renaissance humanism

Sophie Ward

Routledge
Taylor & Francis Group

LONDON AND NEW YORK

First published 2017
by Routledge
2 Park Square, Milton Park, Abingdon, Oxon OX14 4RN

and by Routledge
711 Third Avenue, New York, NY 10017

First issued in paperback 2018

Routledge is an imprint of the Taylor & Francis Group, an informa business

© 2017 Sophie Ward

The right of Sophie Ward to be identified as author of this work has been asserted by her in accordance with sections 77 and 78 of the Copyright, Designs and Patents Act 1988.

All rights reserved. No part of this book may be reprinted or reproduced or utilised in any form or by any electronic, mechanical, or other means, now known or hereafter invented, including photocopying and recording, or in any information storage or retrieval system, without permission in writing from the publishers.

Trademark notice: Product or corporate names may be trademarks or registered trademarks, and are used only for identification and explanation without intent to infringe.

British Library Cataloguing in Publication Data
A catalogue record for this book is available from the British Library

Library of Congress Cataloging in Publication Data
Names: Ward, Sophie, author.
Title: Using Shakespeare's plays to explore education policy today :
    neoliberalism through the lens of Renaissance humanism /
    Sophie Ward.
Description: Abingdon, Oxon ; New York, NY : Routledge, 2017. |
    Includes index.
Identifiers: LCCN 2016025152 | ISBN 9781138903548 (hardcover) |
    ISBN 9781315696850 (electronic)
Subjects: LCSH: Education—Economic aspects. | Education and
    state. | Capitalism and education. | Neoliberalism. | Shakespeare,
William, 1564–1616—Criticism and interpretation.
Classification: LCC LC65 .W34 2017 | DDC 338.4/737—dc23
LC record available at https://lccn.loc.gov/2016025152

ISBN 13: 978-1-138-60257-1 (pbk)
ISBN 13: 978-1-138-90354-8 (hbk)

Typeset in Galliard
by Apex CoVantage, LLC

In loving memory of Claire Louise Aylett
1978–2013

Contents

Acknowledgements   ix

Introduction   1

1   Entrepreneurial risk: *Hamlet*   13

2   Performativity: *Measure for Measure*   30

3   School leadership: *Macbeth*   44

4   Rational choice: *Antony and Cleopatra*   58

5   Commodification: *King Lear*   69

6   Knowledge: *The Tempest*   84

Conclusion   101

Plot summaries   109
Index   117

Acknowledgements

First, I would like to thank my father David Conduct for sharing with me his knowledge of the neoliberal reform of education during his teaching career. My father's views on education inspired me to become a lecturer in education, and this book would not have been written without him. For their love and support I would like to thank my mother Margaret Conduct; my partner Anthony Paul; my son Samuel Ward and my brothers Peter and Matthew Conduct. Lastly, I would like to thank my friend Claire Aylett for the happiness she brought to us all – this book is written as a small tribute to her.

For permission to quote from material to which they control the copyright I am grateful to the following: The University of Chicago Press for F.A. Hayek's *The Constitution of Liberty. The Definitive Edition.* Hamowy, R. (ed.); Simon & Brown for John Dewey's *Democracy and Education*; Harper Collins for *The Meditations of the Emperor Marcus Aurelius Antonius*, Long, G. (trans.); Routledge for Paul Ramsden's *Learning to Lead in Higher Education*; Taylor & Francis Group Ltd. for Todd Whitaker's *What Great Principals Do Differently: 18 Things That Matter Most.* I am grateful to Wiley-Blackwell for permission to reprint as Chapter 4 'Education Under the Heel of Caesar: Reading UK Higher Education Reform through Shakespeare's *Antony and Cleopatra*' by Ward, S.C. (2012) *Journal of Philosophy of Education*, *46* (4), pp. 619–630. Quotations from Shakespeare's plays are from PlayShakespeare.com.

Introduction

William Shakespeare is revered internationally as the greatest playwright in the English language, yet education reform in the English speaking world is informed primarily by the market order promoted by economists such as Friedrich von Hayek and Milton Friedman, rather than the kind of humanism we might associate with Shakespeare. This is significant, as the economic theory that guides contemporary education policy draws upon ideas about the self and society that are rejected by Shakespeare in his plays. For example, *Antony and Cleopatra* exposes the aridity of social theory that denies the value of irrationality, *Macbeth* reveals the danger of moral flexibility and *King Lear* challenges the wisdom of commodification. The utility of Shakespeare's plays as means to explore our present socio-economic system has long been acknowledged and stems from Shakespeare's location at the junction between feudalism and capitalism: writing against this breach, Renaissance playwrights were uniquely positioned to reflect upon the nascent market order.[1] In addition, the study of Shakespeare's plays enables us to interrogate the Renaissance values that are considered by Hayek to be foundational to the neoliberal project.[2] Since the banking crisis of 2007–08, there has been mounting concern over governance in states that have embraced neoliberal policy. Various writers have attempted to explain the increasing gulf between rich and poor; home owners and renters; the educated and those who lack access to education (see for example Noam Chomsky's discussion of social tensions,[3] Thomas Piketty's analysis of the market order[4] and Stephen Ball's critique of neoliberal education reform).[5] Although these writers identify the practical shortcomings of neoliberal economic policy and articulate their objections to what Michael Sandel describes as neoliberalism's dehumanising and debasing social policy,[6] the basis of the ideas they identify as hazardous remains hazy.

Neoliberalism arguably finds it fullest expression through education policy: in the words of John Dewey, 'The most penetrating definition of philosophy which can be given is . . . that it is the theory of education in its most general phases'.[7] In the UK, USA, Australia and New Zealand – indeed everywhere that has implemented the market order after Hayek – there is a growing sense that, to paraphrase *Hamlet*, 'something is wrong in the state of education'. In Australia, John Smyth has urged researchers to critically engage with the neoliberal philosophy informing education reform,[8] yet the diagnosis of what is wrong with the market mechanism has proved difficult to establish, and governments press on with neo-liberal policy implementation. This book aims to clarify what is wrong with the market mechanism by offering a reading of neoliberal theory through some of Shakespeare's plays. In so doing, I hope to demonstrate that the alleged innovation of the market order is premised upon ideas that are rejected by Shakespeare, and to posit Shakespeare's humanism as a corrective to neoliberalism. This book draws upon examples of education policy from the UK and North America, but the international 'paradigm convergence'[9] on neoliberalism means that variations on these policies are found across the world.

I begin by offering a brief account of neoliberalism and Shakespeare's Renaissance humanism. I then provide an overview of the chapters of this book.

Neoliberalism

It is said that UK Prime Minister Margaret Thatcher once tossed Hayek's *The Constitution of Liberty* onto a table and declared '*This* is what we believe'.[10] Hayek has been described as the 'father of neoliberalism',[11] an economic creed that has come to dominate the political and educational landscape of the UK and USA since Thatcher's election in 1979 and President Reagan's election in 1980. Central to Hayek's philosophy is his love of liberty and his dread of social planning, sentiments echoed by Thatcher in her famous assertion that 'There is no such thing as society'[12] and Reagan's jibe that the most terrifying words in the English language are, 'I'm from the government and I'm here to help'.[13] Hayek's revulsion over the empowerment of so-called experts feels intuitively sound: what gives social planners the right to make policy that affects my life, when their perspective is only partial and biased? Is it not better for me to express my preferences as I do every day in the marketplace, and make rational choices according to my intimate knowledge of my personal needs and desires, and for a "social choice" to be the sum of everyone's choices, rather than the will of "experts" imposed on the multitude?

Hayek's own answer to these questions would seem, however, to contradict his argument that the market mechanism empowers individuals. Rather than advocate anarchy, Hayek proposed a form of governance that places tradition at the heart of political decision-making,[14] and we might note here that Shakespeare is pre-eminent in the tradition central to Hayek's market order. Under Hayek's model, experts do not plan our social world: instead, law and order are maintained through the observance of custom, and change is part of an evolutionary process that leads to spontaneous order rather than revolution.[15] Hayek acknowledged that custom may result in the inheritance of land, status and wealth for members of one family and poverty for another, yet he claimed that if we are free to express our preferences within society, rather than obliged to live our lives according to a totalitarian design, then the unequal distribution of resources is acceptable.[16] In Hayek's vision, we are immersed in a tradition that informs the expression of our preferences, and it is this ability to express our preferences – rather than the material gains made through the exercise of free choice – that defines liberty.

A rival theory of free choice was offered by Hayek's contemporary, Ayn Rand, the highly acclaimed 'goddess of the market',[17] who proposed that human reason, rather than tradition, is the bedrock of civilisation. For Rand, laissez-faire capitalism is the highest expression of our capacity for moral reasoning, and liberty is not possible without this exercise of reason, making *non*-thinkers – rich and poor alike – susceptible to tyranny. Again, we might note that Shakespeare has been hailed as the inventor of modern subjectivity[18] and the kind of individuality admired by Rand. Hayek and Rand, alongside other economists and philosophers such as Milton Friedman and James M. Buchanan, shared the conviction that the expression of free choice in the market of goods and services, as postulated by the Enlightenment liberal Adam Smith, inures us to the totalitarian forces of fascism and communism and prevents our descent into anarchy. In spite of their sometimes extreme divergence of opinion on social policy, these "new liberals" forged a beguiling vision of the market society of free individuals expressing their preferences through the market mechanism.

When employing the word "neoliberal", it should be noted that this term is something of an 'academic catchphrase'[19] that is most often used to denigrate the creation of markets, rather than a label applied by economists and philosophers such as Hayek and Rand to describe their own ideas. Although neoliberalism has many variants and could not be described as a 'single system',[20] Taylor Boas and Jordan Gans-Morse have analysed academics' use of the word "neoliberal" in studies of political economy, and have found some consistency in its use to denote (i) economic policy focussed on deregulation and privatisation; (ii) developmental policy focussed on the relationship between private enterprise and the state; (iii) ideology centred upon individual freedom; (iv) positive assumptions about how markets operate.[21] There exists a plethora of competing terms to describe the four areas of debate identified above, such as neoclassical economics, neo-conservativism, New Right thinking, free market fundamentalism and the social market economy. In this book I employ the word neoliberalism to describe the celebration of the market mechanism by diverse writers on political economy.

Shakespeare's Renaissance humanism

Like neoliberalism, Renaissance humanism was not a single school of thought but instead consisted of multiple outlooks that coalesced around what Hanna Gray describes as 'the pursuit of eloquence'.[22] According to Gray, the Renaissance interpretation of classical rhetoric provided the humanists with a 'body of precepts for the effective communication of ideas'[23] and 'a set of principles which asserted the central role of rhetorical skill and achievement in human affairs'.[24] Gray points out that the Renaissance humanists did not equate rhetoric with Sophistry, which they viewed as a perversion of oratory. Instead, they aspired after 'true eloquence', defined as 'a harmonious union between wisdom and style'[25] that will 'guide men toward virtue and worthwhile goals'.[26] The term "humanist" refers to the *studia humanitatis*, or the liberal arts, which comprised the study of grammar, rhetoric, poetry, history, and moral philosophy.[27] Renaissance humanists such as Thomas More and Desiderius Erasmus believed that the aim of liberal education is not to prepare the individual for a specific activity or profession, but to 'enhance the possibilities of being human'.[28] Shakespeare attended the King's New School in Stratford, and Stephen Greenblatt notes that his plays are 'laced with echoes of many of the great Latin texts taught in grammar schools'.[29] Shakespeare did not, however, attend university and was not considered to be highly educated by the standards of his day.[30] Famously, Shakespeare's friend Ben Jonson remarked in his statement in the First Folio that Shakespeare had 'small *Latine*, and lesse *Greeke*'.[31] In his lifetime, Shakespeare was regarded as an entertainer rather than a philosopher, and David Bevington argues that this is why we have no contemporary biographies of him and so few examples of his handwriting.[32] 'Sophisticated readers', says Bevington, 'did not ordinarily 'collect' Shakespeare'.[33] However, in spite of Shakespeare's relatively modest study of the liberal arts, few disputed that Shakespeare's plays combined 'wisdom and style'[34] to explore the possibilities of being human, and thus conformed to the humanists' definition of 'true eloquence'.[35] In the words of Jonson, Shakespeare was the 'Soule of the Age!'[36]

Today, deliberation on the status of Shakespeare's Renaissance humanism is somewhat fraught. Reflecting on the 'culture wars' of the 1980s, Todd Gitlin argues that the political Right in the USA once stood for the interests of the few, while the Left identified with the universal condition of the masses.[37] According to Gitlin, this position was inverted in the late twentieth century when the Right appropriated the language of universal values and "common sense", and the Left became entangled in identity politics around race, gender, sexuality and so on, which focused attention on difference and undermined collective identity and a sense of common purpose. For cultural critics, this inversion was perhaps most apparent with regard to Shakespeare. Traditionally, left-wing writers such as Karl Marx viewed Shakespeare's plays through the prism of Jonson's claim that Shakespeare 'was not of an age, but for all time!'[38] As noted by Richard Levin, Shakespeare's denigration of 'the kind of individualism and acquisitiveness that came to be associated with capitalism'[39] was viewed by Marx as a timeless appeal to common sense. Levin claims that both Shakespeare and Marx had a tendency to 'idealize feudalism'[40] as a buffer to the instrumentality of capitalism, and Marx's ostensible willingness to endorse Shakespeare's position on social stratification proved distasteful to subsequent left-wing scholars. During the countercultural revolution of the 1960s and 1970s, cultural materialism emerged as a new method of engagement with literary works that sought to acknowledge that 'no cultural practice is ever without political significance'.[41] By focussing on art as the expression of ideology, left-wing critics were able to engage with the complexity of Shakespeare's thought without appearing to endorse what they saw as the Western imperialist assumption that Renaissance humanism is the universal perspective of humankind. According to Jonathan Dollimore and Alan Sinfield:

> A play by Shakespeare is related to the contexts of its production – to the economic and political system of Elizabethan and Jacobean England and

to the particular institutions of cultural production (the court, patronage, theatre, education, the church). Moreover, the relevant history is not just that of four hundred years ago, for culture is made continuously and Shakespeare's text is reconstructed, reappraised, reassigned all the time through diverse institutions in specific contexts. What the plays signify, how they signify, depends on the cultural field in which they are situated.[42]

Excitement over the possibilities of "resignification" led to an explosion of diverse readings of Shakespeare's work aligned with identity politics, such as Mahadi Menon's *Shakesqueer: A Queer Companion to the Complete Works of Shakespeare*;[43] Dympna Callaghan's *Feminist Companion to Shakespeare*,[44] and Ania Loomba's *Shakespeare, Race and Colonialism*.[45] In addition to this cornucopia of "identity studies" of Shakespeare, cultural materialism led to the emergence of New Economic Criticism to explore what Bertolt Brecht identified as Shakespeare's tragic rendition of the decline of feudalism and the rise of the capitalist state.[46] By articulating the distinction between such things as use-value and exchange-value, books like *Money and the Age of Shakespeare* have enabled readers to access the Renaissance world of commerce that is dramatized by Shakespeare and to appreciate the enormity of change wrought by capitalism.[47]

For conservative cultural critics, however, left-wing resignification seems to imply that our understanding of Shakespeare is contingent upon our ephemeral and circumscribed vantage point, rather than our recognition of the timeless values enshrined in his plays. During the culture wars, a concerted effort was therefore made to reassert the universality of Shakespeare as the pre-eminent writer on the human condition. For example, in *Shakespeare: the Invention of the Human*, Harold Bloom argues that Bardolatry 'ought to be even more a secular religion than it already is'[48] on the grounds that Shakespeare's plays are the highest expression of human cognition, creativity, morality and spirituality. According to Bloom, Shakespeare is not only fundamental to the Western canon, but also to the world's 'implicit canon',[49] and he cites the worldwide fascination with Shakespeare as evidence of a power within his plays that cannot be constrained by parochial readings that seek either to contextualise Shakespeare or to re-signify his art. In his analysis of the culture wars, Michael Bristol argues that the teaching of Shakespeare has been used by conservatives to expound the view that 'there are overarching values that usefully transcend the parochialism of identity politics';[50] a view endorsed more recently by Kieran Ryan, who claims that Shakespeare's plays assume a 'common humanity'.[51] According to Ryan, Shakespeare's dramas reveal how we might base our lives together 'on values that possess universal validity, because they are founded on the simple, irrefutable fact that we belong to the same species'.[52] Such resistance to the apparent denial of our common humanity wrought by identity politics has, at times, been accompanied by hostility towards neoliberal marketisation. For example, Helen Gardner's *In Defence of the Imagination* is cited by Bristol as an illustration of the conservatives' call-to-arms to study great literature to resist the reduction of society to 'a mere ant-heap'[53] devoted to the mindless accumulation of wealth.

This observation is perhaps surprising, as Hayek and his followers within conservative governments in the UK and USA have positioned traditional values as fundamental to the operation of the market society, and we might therefore expect condemnation of marketisation to come from the Left, rather than the Right. According to Stuart Hall, conservatives' response to neoliberalism has been vexed, and he argues that neoliberal politicians have attempted to marry the conservative defence of common humanity with the pursuit of economic self-interest by aligning neoliberal economic reform with nostalgia for past glory.[54] The neoliberal celebration of 'the flag, family values, national character, imperial glory and the spirit of . . . gunboat diplomacy'[55] has thus gone hand-in-glove with what Graham Holderness describes as the 'relic-worship'[56] of Shakespeare as a valuable component of the UK's tourist industry.

What, then, of left-wing objections to neoliberalism? No longer comfortable with the concept of universality, socialist critics have condemned the 'ant-heap' existence as an affront to social justice from the vantage point of particular groups (for example, the impact of neoliberal education reform on ethnic minority pupils) or from the vantage point of particular effects (for example, the impact of neoliberal education reform on pupils' mental health). Today, left-wing writers are unlikely to prescribe Shakespeare's Renaissance humanism as a panacea to neoliberalism, as this would validate feudal social stratification – an endorsement which is, of course, irreconcilable with identity politics. In this book, I adopt a methodology inspired by New Economic Criticism to consider Shakespeare's response to capitalism's 'ant-heap' ethos, and to reflect upon contemporary response to the implementation of neoliberal education policy. In so doing, my aim is not to idealise feudalism, but instead to point to the common ground between left-wing and right-wing critics of neoliberalism who object to the vacuity of life based solely on the accumulation of capital. The plays selected for analysis in this book consist of four tragedies, one romance and a comedy. According to Louis Montrose, the 'dominant social institutions and cultural practices'[57] in Shakespeare's day were 'predicated upon an ideology of unchanging order and absolute obedience',[58] yet Elizabethan and Jacobean theatre was 'still imbued with the heritage of suppressed popular and religious traditions'.[59] It is predominantly through the medium of tragedy that Shakespeare explores what Montrose identifies as the suppression of institutions and practices under the emergent capitalist system, yet Shakespeare's comedy, *Measure for Measure* offers what might be described as the most biting critique of the shift from medieval to modern modalities of power. Given the censorship of plays at this time, Shakespeare's use of comedy for this purpose was no doubt politic. In the saying attributed to Oscar Wilde, 'If you want to tell people the truth, make them laugh, otherwise they'll kill you'. It is my contention that Shakespeare's humanism is a corrective to neoliberalism, not because his plays advocate what many consider to be an unattractive medieval social order, but because his challenge to capitalism enables us to maintain our connection with a host of ideas about the self and society that are in danger of being stifled by the 'mono-discourse'[60] of neoliberalism. Milton Friedman, one of neoliberalism's chief architects, famously declared that it was his intention to watch and wait for neoliberalism's moment to come, keeping alive alternate policies during the long years of Keynesian economics until the moment when 'the politically impossible becomes politically inevitable'.[61] We might fruitfully do the same: by keeping alive alternatives to neoliberalism through our study of Shakespeare, we too may be ready to capitalise upon what Friedman describes as 'a crisis – actual or perceived'[62] that enables us to overcome the 'tyranny of the status quo'.[63]

***

Chapter 1 *Entrepreneurial risk:* Hamlet

This chapter introduces the concept of the neoliberal entrepreneur as a hero who is willing to bear risk in the market society, yet is constrained by bureaucracy. During the 1980s, fascination with entrepreneurialism was mixed with fear that the irrationality of the permissive society might minimise the potential to be heroic. In previous decades, economists had identified the entrepreneur as the vital everyman of the market society who embodies the kind of rationality that critics have attributed to *Hamlet* as the depiction of 'the first modern man'.[64] By considering the neoliberal idea of the heroic entrepreneur through a reading of *Hamlet*, this chapter reflects upon the idea of rationality which is fundamental to the neoliberal project, and considers Buchanan's theory of anarchy from the perspective of this play. The subtlety of Shakespeare's depiction of rationality is considered in light of Weber's claim that charisma is a force that disrupts rational rule and tradition, making it antithetical to both Rand's theory that the market order is based on the exercise of reason and Hayek's belief that it is dependent upon tradition. This chapter argues that neoliberal education policy is designed to make pupils embrace risk in the market society by gaining credentials for employment, and is therefore oppositional to the emotional life of Hamlet the scholar, as it sustains the market order and suppresses charismatic disruption.

Chapter 2 *Performativity:* Measure for Measure

This chapter considers how exponents of neoliberalism have attempted to eradicate the educational manifestation of the permissive society by supplanting progressive education with tradition through a process that Foucault describes as the direction of 'gaze'. The theoretical basis of this project is explored through an analysis of both the conservative and socialist response to the irrationality of fascistic altruism during the Second World War and Hayek's deliberation on why state education is *not* a totalitarian activity. The contemporary desire to make teachers self-regulate as neoliberal subjects through a process described by Stephen Ball as 'the terror of performativity' is considered in light of Shakespeare's depiction of governance in *Measure for Measure*. In so doing, the modalities of power identified by Foucault – external rational control and internal subjective policing – are made visible. Consideration of *Measure for Measure*'s happy ending, which is dependent upon the willingness of those in power to recognise the value of human relations and to modify their governance accordingly, suggests that neoliberalism's victory over progressivism is likely to be won at the expense of human connectivity unless a similar concession is made.

Chapter 3 School leadership: Macbeth

Hayek identified the Renaissance as the source of our 'respect for the individual man *qua* man'.[65] Antony Jay also took inspiration from the Renaissance in his book, *Management and Machiavelli*, which helped popularise Machiavelli's Renaissance leadership theory contemporaneously with the ascension of neoliberalism. Today, educators praise Machiavelli's pragmatism, saying he looked at what worked instead of trying to identify what was right or wrong. This view is consistent with Hayek's belief that progress is made possible through individuals' cooperation with abstract rules of conduct, rather than compliance with concrete common aims. According to Hayek, the market mechanism precludes the imposition of one person's will over another, making marketised relations under New Public Management ethically neutral. This supposition is challenged through a reading of *Macbeth*, in which Machiavelli's moral flexibility is shown to violate natural and divine law and undermine human connectivity. Seen in light of *Macbeth*, school leadership for equity is an unlikely vehicle for social justice, as it aligns success with school leaders' ability to employ knowledge to enhance the position of their schools in performance league tables, making school leadership contingent upon the pursuit of the same self-interest critiqued by Shakespeare.

Chapter 4 Rational choice: Antony and Cleopatra

Hayek argued that rationalist planning can never be truly effective or efficient as such planning is dependent upon imperfect information, and advocated instead the expression of individuals' free choice via the market mechanism to yield what he described as spontaneous order or equilibrium. Hayek's theory was challenged by Buchanan, who believed that efficiency should be engineered, rather than left to chance. Consistent with Buchanan's Public Choice theory, higher education reform in England has been presented as a movement towards efficiency, engineered by government but operationally dependent upon students' exercise of rational choice in the education marketplace. This chapter argues that, in reality, the marketisation of higher education is a movement towards negative liberty, defined after Isaiah Berlin as unrestricted choice. By offering a reading of English higher education reform through *Antony and Cleopatra* and comparing Shakespeare's drama with Nietzsche's theory of Apollonian individuation and Dionysian unity, this chapter considers how negative liberty, far from functioning as a panacea to inefficiency, risks undermining human connectivity and debasing our relationships.

Chapter 5 Commodification: King Lear

Commodification is the process through which phenomena are evaluated according to their exchange value in the context of trade. In the field of education, this value is identified through research into "what works". To its supporters, school effectiveness research (SER) seems to offer the potential to maximise educational performance by modelling within-school complexities. To its critics, however, SER provides the mechanism for comparative data that consumers need to make markets work. This chapter asks if commodification is *inevitable* through a reading of the commodification of love in *King Lear*. In this play, Shakespeare appears to contrast the Stoics' faith in universal natural law with Machiavellianism, and compare the general (gift-exchange) economy and the restricted (market-exchange) economy. Analysis of *King Lear* seems to imply that the equilibrium of the market society is predicated upon the disavowal of the collective gift of nature's bounty and the acceptance of the theory of scarcity. This chapter argues that the purpose of commodification is to facilitate pupils' market participation, rather than ensure equality of life outcome. The fear of having and being "nothing" is, it seems, fundamental to the neoliberal model of education and underpins our anxiety over the accruement of credentials for employment. Although not inevitable, commodification is likely to continue unless we are prepared to remove the rentier entrepreneur from the pedestal of hero and to disavow the mythology of risk in the market society.

Chapter 6 Knowledge: The Tempest

The classical theory of liberal education rested upon the notion that knowledge is the understanding of reality. In contrast, the pragmatist philosopher William James argued that our responsiveness to a hypothesis is not dependent upon its intrinsic properties, but upon its relationship to our existing beliefs and proclivities. John Dewey's pragmatist account of education, which rejected the idea that knowledge is simply the beholding of reality, developed into the theory of constructivism, which holds that knowledge is an organisation of concepts, expectations and abilities that enables successful coping with the world. Through a reading of *The Tempest*, this chapter problematises both Shakespeare's depiction of Aristotle's concept of liberal education and Dewey's rejection of this concept, and considers how neoliberalism has capitalised upon constructivist accounts of knowledge to position economic self-actualisation as the end of education. Drawing upon Illich's theory of deschooling as a means to create utopia, this chapter argues that while there is no easy answer to the question, 'What is education for?' we cut off hope of cultivating a society that aims for anything higher than the accumulation of wealth if we concede to the neoliberal view that education is simply about gaining skills and credentials for employment.

Notes

1 Hawkes, D. (2015) *Shakespeare and Economic Theory*. London: Bloomsbury Publishing Plc.
2 Hayek, F.A. (2007) *The Road to Serfdom. Text and Documents: The Definitive Edition*. Chicago: The University of Chicago Press.
3 Chomsky, N. (2012) *Occupy*. London: Penguin Books Ltd.
4 Piketty, T. (2014) *Capital in the Twenty-First Century*. London: The Belknap Press of Harvard University Press.
5 Ball, S.J. (2012) *Global Education Inc*. Abingdon: Routledge.
6 Sandel, M. (2012) *What Money Can't Buy: The Moral Limits of Markets*. London: Allen Lane.
7 Dewey, J. (2011) *Democracy and Education*. www.simonandbrown.com, p. 180.
8 Smyth, J. (2008) 'Australia's Great Disengagement with Public Education and Social Justice in Educational Leadership' *Journal of Educational Administration and History*, *40* (3), pp. 221–233.
9 Ball, S.J. (2001: 48) 'Labour, Learning and the Economy: A "Policy Sociology" Perspective' In: Fielding, M. (ed.) *Taking Education Really Seriously: Four Years Hard Labour*. London: RoutledgeFalmer. pp. 45–56.
10 Marquand, D. (2014) *Mammon's Kingdom: An Essay on Britain, Now*. London: Allen Lane. p. 106.
11 Boneau, D. (2004) 'Friedrich von Hayek, the Father of Neoliberalism' *Voltaire Network, Paris (France)*. Available online at: http://www.voltairenet.org/article 30058.html [Accessed 11th April 2016].
12 Margaret Thatcher (1987) Interview for *Women's Own*. Available online at: http://www.margaretthatcher.org/document/106689 [Accessed 16th April 2015].
13 Reagan, R. (1986) 'The President's news conference, August 12th 1986'. Available online at: http://www.reaganfoundation.org/reagan-quotes-detail.aspx?tx=2079 [Accessed 3rd September 2015].
14 Posner, R. A. (2005) 'Hayek, Law and Cognition' *N.Y.U. Journal of Law & Liberty*, *1*, pp. 147–166.
15 Hayek, F.A. (2011) *The Constitution of Liberty: The Definitive Edition*. Hamowy, R. (ed.). Chicago: The University of Chicago Press.
16 Hayek (2007).
17 Burns, J. (2009) *Goddess of the Market: Ayn Rand and the American Right*. Oxford: Oxford University Press.
18 Bloom, H. (1999) *Shakespeare: The Invention of the Human*. London: Fourth Estate.
19 Boas, T.C. & Gans-Morse, J. (2009: 137) 'Neoliberalism: From New Liberal Philosophy to Anti-Liberal Slogan' *St Comp Int Dev*, *44*, pp. 137–161.
20 Hall, S. (2011: 708) 'The Neo-Liberal Revolution' *Cultural Studies*, *25* (6), pp. 705–728.
21 Boas & Gans-Morse (2009: 137).
22 Gray, H.H. (1963: 498) 'Renaissance Humanism: The Pursuit of Eloquence' *Journal of the History of Ideas*, *24* (4), pp. 497–514.
23 Ibid.
24 Ibid.
25 Ibid.
26 Ibid.
27 Ibid: 499.
28 Baker-Smith, D. (2014) 'Thomas More', *The Stanford Encyclopaedia of Philosophy*. Spring 2014 Edition, Edward N. Zalta (ed.). Available online at: http://plato.stanford.edu/archives/spr2014/entries/thomas-more/ [Accessed 12th April 2016].

29 Greenblatt, S. (1997: 44) 'General Introduction' In: *The Norton Shakespeare*. New York, NY: W.W. Norton & Company, Inc. pp. 1–76.

30 Burrow, C. (2013) *Shakespeare and Classical Antiquity*. Oxford: Oxford University Press.

31 Jonson, B. in Baldwin, T.W. (1944) *William Shakspere's Small Latine & Lesse Greeke*. Urbana: University of Illinois Press. p. 2.

32 Bevington, D. (2008) *Shakespeare's Ideas: More Things in Heaven and Earth*. Chichester: Wiley-Blackwell.

33 Ibid: 5.

34 Gray (1963: 498).

35 Ibid.

36 Jonson in Baldwin (ibid).

37 Gitlin, T. (1995) *The Twilight of Common Dreams: Why America is Wracked By Culture Wars*. New York: Metropolitan Books.

38 Jonson in Baldwin (ibid).

39 Levin, R. (1991: 53) 'Reply to Michael Bristol and Gayle Green' In: Kamps, I. (ed.) *Shakespeare Left and Right*. New York: Routledge. pp. 47–60.

40 Ibid.

41 Dollimore, J. & Sinfield, A. (2003: viii) 'Foreword' In: Dollimore, J. & Sinfield, A. (eds.) *Political Shakespeare: Essays in Cultural Materialism*. Second Edition. Manchester: Manchester University Press. pp. vii–viii.

42 Ibid.

43 Menon, M. (2011) (ed.) *Shakesqueer: A Queer Companion to the Complete Works of Shakespeare*. Durham & London: Duke University Press.

44 Callaghan, D. (2001) (ed.) *A Feminist Companion to Shakespeare*. Oxford: Blackwell Publishers Ltd.

45 Loomba, A. (2002) *Shakespeare, Race, and Colonialism*. Oxford: Oxford University Press.

46 Heinemann, M. (2003) 'How Brecht Read Shakespeare' In: Dollimore, J. & Sinfield, A. (eds.) *Political Shakespeare: Essays in Cultural Materialism*. Second Edition. Manchester: Manchester University Press. pp. 226–254.

47 Woodbridge, L. (2003) (ed.) *Money and the Age of Shakespeare*. Basingstoke: Palgrave Machmillan.

48 Bloom (1999: xvii).

49 Ibid: 717.

50 Bristol, M.D. (1996) *Big-Time Shakespeare*. London: Routledge. p. 21.

51 Ryan, K. (2015) *Shakespeare's Universality: Here's Fine Revolution*. London: Bloomsbury Arden Shakespeare. p. 11.

52 Ibid: 10.

53 Gardner, H. in Bristol (1996: 17).

54 Hall (2011).

55 Ibid: 713.

56 Holderness, G. (2001) *Cultural Shakespeare: Essays in the Shakespeare Myth*. Hatfield: University of Hertfordshire Press. p. 126.

57 Montrose, L. (1996) *The Purpose of Playing: Shakespeare and the Cultural Politics of the Elizabethan Theatre*. Chicago: University of Chicago Press. p. 39.

58 Ibid.

59 Ibid.

60 Ward, S.C. (2014: 83) 'Education and the "New Totalitarianism": How Standards for Reporting on Empirical Studies of Education Limit the Scope of Academic Research and Communication' In: Smeyers P. & Depaepe M. (eds.) *Educational Research: Material Culture and Its Representation*. Dordrecht: Springer. pp. 71–85.

61 Friedman, M. (2002) *Capitalism and Freedom: 40th Anniversary Edition.* Chicago: University of Chicago Press. p. xiv.

62 Ibid.

63 Ibid.

64 Rossiter, A.P. (1961: 187) *Angel with Horns and Other Shakespeare Lectures.* New York: Theatre Arts Books.

65 Hayek, F.A. (2007: 68).

1 Entrepreneurial risk

Hamlet

Introduction

During the 1980s, Sir Keith Joseph was the UK's Secretary of State for Education. Known as the 'mad monk',[1] Joseph played a central role in the neoliberal transformation of the Conservative Party under Margaret Thatcher, to whom he introduced the works of F.A. Hayek, and was considered to be 'a Saint or Satan',[2] depending on one's political outlook. Joseph's philosophy of education was informed by his fascination with entrepreneurialism, which he shared with other notable figures of the day such as John Kao of Harvard Business School and the US writer Ayn Rand. Joseph's biographers, Andrew Denham and Mark Garnett, record Joseph's admiration for the man or woman who 'begins with nothing' and achieves apparently magical success; a 'mystery' explored in one of his last speeches where he mused, 'They do not come because of good education and they do not come of good birth. They do not come because of happy homes or unhappy homes. We do not know how they come . . .'[3] Joseph's anti-cultural theory of entrepreneurialism was curiously at odds with his hatred for Jean-Jacques Rousseau's theory of 'natural' education, which he believed had encouraged twentieth-century teachers 'to dispense with the structured systems of learning which have been so successful in the past' and promoted the belief 'that a permissive society is a civilised society'.[4] In Chapter 2 of this book I discuss the attempt to eradicate progressive education in the UK and North America, and as a prelude to that discussion this current chapter considers the impulse *towards* that endeavour by asking, 'Who is this 'entrepreneur' so beloved of neoliberals? How is her power non-attributable to her genes, her upbringing or her education, yet potentially nullified by the "permissive society"?'

In seeking to untangle this central knot of neoliberal philosophy, I offer a reading of Shakespeare's *Hamlet*, whose eponymous hero is described by A.P. Rossiter as 'the first modern man'.[5] According to Stephen Greenblatt, *Hamlet* marks an 'epochal shift'[6] not only in Shakespeare's writing, but in Western drama itself. By employing 'dramatic poetry and prose of unprecedented intensity'[7] in this play, Shakespeare introduced a 'whole new kind of literary subjectivity'[8] based on the feeling of being inside a character's psyche. This subjectivity inspired the Shakespeare cult of the Romantic era,[9] when the idea of transcendence through introspection exploded the Enlightenment notion of rationality as the pre-eminent guide to human action. Hamlet's tortuous soul-searching provided the template for Romantic depictions of social misfits, such as Johann Wolfgang von Goethe's, *The Sorrows of Young Werther*, and established the literary trope of the sensitive thinker struggling to cope in a world of phlegmatic doers. At first glance, *Hamlet* appears an unlikely blueprint for the neoliberal "go-getter", yet it paved the way for both Romantic mysticism and the rejection of this route of travel in the form of Rand's Market-Romantic philosophy, and the play's depiction of rationality and tradition arguably provides a useful lens through which to scrutinise neoliberal theory on volition and entrepreneurialism.

Hamlet

Hamlet reveals the chasm between the worlds of the 'warrior-king and modern humanist'[10] and thus gives epic scale to the issue of volition. These worlds collide most forcibly when the ghost of Hamlet's father appears before his grieving son dressed in full battle armour and discloses that his brother murdered him to steal the crown and marry Hamlet's mother. Deeply impressed by his father's clamorous demand for remembrance and retaliation, Hamlet vows to forget the precepts of humanism acquired through study at Wittenberg University, declaring:

> Yea, from the table of my memory
> I'll wipe away all trivial fond records,
> All saws of books, all forms, all pressures past
> That youth and observation copied there,
> And thy commandment all alone shall live
> Within the book and volume of my brain,
> Unmix'd with baser matter.
>
> (1.5.98–104)

This promise proves easier to make than keep. Instead of getting on with the business of revenge, Hamlet finds himself enthusiastically recalling lines from classical drama with a troupe of actors, and is subsequently plunged into a fit of self-loathing, proclaiming, 'O vengeance! / Why, what an ass am I!' (2.2.579–580). In spite of his vow to forsake the arts and his disgust at his own vacillation, Hamlet goes on to philosophise that the apparition of his father may have been a devil conjured 'Out of my weakness and my melancholy' (2.2.599), and decides to test his uncle's guilt by staging a pantomime of his father's murder, thereby further delaying the act of retaliation. Appearing before his son a second time, the ghost of Hamlet's father urges remembrance saying, 'Do not forget! This visitation / Is but to whet thy almost blunted purpose' (3.4.111–112). Hamlet's soliloquies reveal, however, not that he has forgotten his murderous mission, but that he finds it difficult to think without employing methods cultivated through humanist study. We might, of course, agree with Hamlet that it is *reasonable* to test the hypothesis that the ghost is a devil sent to trick him, and indeed the wisdom of such careful reflection is brought home to us at the close of the drama, when we witness Laertes blundering towards his own demise without considering, in advance of action, the possibility that he is being manipulated by the king. Nevertheless, Hamlet's prevarication proves ruinous, and the phlegmatic Fortinbras, who is impervious to the political balderdash that undermines Laertes's chance of power, claims the crown of Denmark with a flourish of chivalric honour that calls to mind the historic seizure of this same land by Hamlet's warrior-father.

Reason and volition

Hamlet is torn between honouring filial obligations and choosing his own values, and however much this "choice" is limited by his prior conditioning, his predicament is illustrative of, and indeed emanates from, his capacity for reason. The nature of this uniquely human capacity is one of the central preoccupations of neoliberal philosophy, and arguably the most interesting writer on this topic is Ayn Rand. In *The Romantic Manifesto*, published in 1969, Rand defines Romanticism as a category of art based on the recognition of our capacity for volition, and she argues that the exercise of free will is a moral act.[11] Arguably, Rand's use of the term 'Romantic' is problematic, as the nineteenth-century Romantic movement was informed by the belief, which Peter Holbrook claims Shakespeare shared with Montaigne and Machiavelli, that reason is of limited help in choosing among values because our 'ultimate values'[12] are often incompatible. This limitation is rejected by Rand, who contrasts *her* brand of Romanticism with "immoral" Naturalism, arguing that exponents of the latter believe that our choices are constrained by forces beyond our control, and that the moral agent is not therefore autonomous. For Rand, Naturalism enervates society by making individuals feel weak, and in her novels she demonstrates her philosophy through the depiction of audacious men and women choosing their values, rather than relying upon social convention or allowing "fate" to guide their action. In addition, Rand discards the old-style Romantic notion that our rationality might be supplemented by supernatural knowledge, arguing that the 'virtue of Rationality'[13] means 'the rejection of any form of *mysticism, i.e.*, any claim to some nonsensory, nonrational, nondefinable, supernatural source of knowledge'.[14] This disinclination to acknowledge the role of mysticism in human affairs is not, of course, limited to neoliberal philosophers such as Rand. The literary theorist Harold Bloom, like his nineteenth-century Romantic predecessors, believes that watching *Hamlet* is an uncanny experience because something about this play seems to both demand and provide 'evidence from some sphere beyond the scope of our senses'.[15] However, Bloom seems to imply that this sphere beyond the scope of our senses is *not* supernatural, but a heightened realm of perception accessed by Shakespeare, who affords us a glimpse of what he sees through Hamlet as his proxy. Thus, Bloom proclaims that consciousness is Hamlet's 'salient characteristic' and that 'he is the most aware and knowing figure ever conceived',[16] in spite of the fact that Hamlet only discovers the regicide that fuels this drama through the mystical intervention of his dead father. Rand goes further than Bloom by offering an interpretation of Hamlet's most famous soliloquy that positions him squarely as a rational thinker, rather than mystical seer. In her novel, *Atlas Shrugged*, the hero John Galt proclaims that man is a *'volitional consciousness'*;[17] a physical entity whose organs function automatically but whose mind must be commanded into action by an effort of will. Without this effort man will die, as he is not born with the knowledge necessary for survival. Consequently, Galt says, 'for *you*, who are a human being, the question 'to be or not to be' is the question 'to think or not to think.'"[18] This implies that not to think is to die, but of course this philosophy is quite different from that expressed by Hamlet, who believes that death may open the door to the unwelcome continuation of thought in the form of uncontrollable dreams.

Rand's Objectivist philosophy, which she describes as the moral base of laissez-faire capitalism,[19] is overtly atheist and has proved deeply attractive to individuals longing for decisive answers to questions about the meaning of life in our more secular age.[20] Other exponents of marketisation have painted portraits of human reasoning that, while less engaging than Rand's "Market Romanticism", perhaps resemble more closely the rationality depicted in *Hamlet*. The US economist, James M. Buchanan, who served as President of the Mont Pelerin Society founded by Friedrich A. Hayek, is best known for his work on Public Choice theory, which he describes as 'policy without romance'.[21] In *The Limits of Liberty*, published in 1975, Buchanan displays unabashed pragmatism over human relations, arguing that 'We live together because social organization provides the efficient means of achieving our objectives and not because society offers us a means of arriving at some transcendental common bliss'.[22] This conjecture calls to mind Hamlet's rejection of humanity as a source of comfort when he tells his erstwhile friends, 'Man delights not me – nor woman neither' (2.2.309). For Hamlet, the social organisation of the Danish court of Elsinore provides neither 'common bliss' nor the efficient means of achieving his objectives; indeed, it thwarts them through constant surveillance (*for more discussion of surveillance, see Chapter 2*).

Buchanan argues that a social system that denies self-actualisation cannot be justified on the spurious grounds that it offers spiritual communion, but he firmly rejects anarchism as an alternative to the kind of 'prison' structure that Hamlet rails against (2.2.243). Using the analogy of Robin Hood and Little John meeting in the middle of a one-man footbridge, Buchanan argues that there is no "natural" rule to determine who is entitled to proceed and who must withdraw: 'The genuinely anarchistic world becomes a maze of footbridges, and conflict rather than universalized cooperation is its central feature'.[23] Hamlet seems to personify this conflict when he finds relief from inertia through impetuous action, randomly stabbing Polonius through a curtain and sending Guildenstern and Rosencrantz to their deaths. To borrow from Buchanan, Hamlet assaults people who are blocking his path on a metaphorical one-man footbridge, and in so doing he violates what Rand describes as the basic political principle of the Objectivist ethic that no person may *initiate* the use of physical force against another.[24] Buchanan, however, denies the possibility of a universal ethic, and argues that the pursuit of individual gain is rational and entirely to be expected, and must therefore be moderated through legislation. For Buchanan, laissez-faire capitalism, with its focus on individual rights and the freedom to make voluntary contracts, is the surest means to both resist anarchy and limit the scope of totalitarian collective power. Even a 'romantic revolutionary'[25] would, he says, prefer order over chaos, and might even acknowledge that 'all members of a community secure gains when rights are defined'.[26] Thus, while Rand argues that our capacity for reason defines us as human and that exercising free choice in the market society enables us to fully realise our humanity, Buchanan adopts a non-Romantic position, arguing that the definition of property rights is the instrument through which a person is initially defined, and that the market mechanism is simply the most efficient means of limiting coercion.

In spite of the broad appeal of Rand and Buchanan's ideas, it was arguably Hayek's theory that established the central ground of neoliberal policy. In *The Constitution of Liberty*, published in 1960, Hayek devotes a chapter to 'Freedom, Reason and Tradition', in which he sets out his position on rationality.[27] Hayek pulls no punches when arguing in favour of the British empirical tradition over the French rationalist tradition, claiming that 'the British philosophers laid the foundations of a profound and essentially valid theory, while the rationalist school was simply and completely wrong.'[28] Hayek claims that the empiricist and rationalist positions are underpinned by two fundamentally different accounts of the human: the anti-rationalist theory is, he says, 'closer to the Christian tradition of the fallibility and sinfulness of man',[29] while the rationalist theory is 'based on the assumption of the individual man's propensity for rational action and his natural intelligence and goodness'.[30] This latter assumption is wrong, he argues, because when making a decision about whether or not to obey rules, we do not know 'what depends on their being observed in the particular instance'[31] and cannot therefore rely upon our capacity for reason to guide us. Although Hayek is sceptical of the 'French tradition, with its flattering assumptions about the unlimited powers of human reason',[32] he does not propose that our reason might be supplemented by supernatural knowledge. Instead, he borrows from Darwin's theory of evolution to argue in favour of the slow, *organic* growth of social convention through a process of trial and error. As in the natural world, he argues, behaviour in the social world is moderated through the "natural selection" of actions that lead to favourable results over time. Hayek claims that the decision to adhere to a moral code 'must be regarded as a value in itself, a sort of intermediate end which we must pursue without questioning its justification in the particular case'.[33] In subsequent work Hayek went on to state that ethical rules are tacit and acquired through imitation, and that the family plays a central role in cultivating the virtues that have evolved to support the Great Society.[34] This philosophy was an anathema to Rand, who believed that ethical truths are objectively knowable and that families risk suffocating this ability by supplanting reason with unthinking filial duty.[35] Buchanan was also sceptical of Hayek's theory of social evolution, arguing that 'the institutions that survive and prosper need not be those that maximise man's potential. Evolution may produce social dilemma as readily as social paradise'.[36]

Charisma and the entrepreneur

The difficulty of reconciling filial duty with the desire for self-determination is central to *Hamlet*, and when considering the Danish court in evolutionary terms we would certainly struggle to describe it as a 'social paradise'. In order to explore the role accorded to tradition in *Hamlet*, it is perhaps helpful to consider Max Weber's analysis of charisma in *Economy and Society*, published posthumously in 1922.[37] We might note here two claims made by Weber that are significant for our study of *Hamlet* and the neoliberal entrepreneur: first that charisma disrupts rational rule, and second that it disrupts tradition, making his definition of charisma antithetical to both Rand's vision of the heroic rationalist and Hayek's vision of the dynamic free market underpinned by tradition. Weber claims that bureaucracy and patriarchalism are both 'oriented toward the satisfaction of calculable needs with ordinary, everyday means',[38] and that extraordinary needs are satisfied on a *charismatic* basis. Thus, two distinct types of need are met through what might be described as a process of regulation and innovation. The bureaucratic or paternalistic figure of authority ("the regulator") is located in a pre-existing control structure: as long as the structure holds and the individual complies with traditional expectations of behaviour, his or her claim to authority is assured. The charismatic figure ("the innovator") is located outside this control structure and demonstrates extraordinary abilities which we are *compelled* to recognise: if these abilities are tested and found wanting, his or her claim to authority vanishes. Weber argues that charisma 'disrupts rational rule as well as tradition altogether and overturns all notions of sanctity'.[39] According to Weber, this charismatic disruption *enhances* our culture, as 'Instead of reverence for customs that are ancient and hence sacred, it enforces the inner subjection to the unprecedented and absolutely unique and therefore Divine'.[40] Instead of evolution, it is revolution that Weber hails: 'In this purely empirical and value-free sense charisma is indeed the specifically creative revolutionary force of history'.[41] Weber's theory that creativity is dependent upon freedom from the rule of reason and tradition constitutes a direct challenge to Hayek's claim that stability through time-honoured tradition is the foundation of a free and vibrant society. Perhaps most strikingly, Weber's theory that charisma is non-economic seems to undermine the rational basis of the free market, as he claims that the charismatic prophet and pirate are equally oblivious to everyday rules and conventions, in spite of their diverse views on the accruement of wealth.

If we find Weber's definition of charisma persuasive, we may decide that Hamlet's father is charismatic because he seized power through a display of valour, rather than diplomacy, and allowed Elsinore's traditions to lapse, so that keeping wassail is 'a custom/More honour'd in the breech than the observance' (1.4.15–16). By this same measure Hamlet is *not* charismatic, as he is desperate to honour traditional filial obligations and is unable to extract himself from the rational rule of Wittenberg scholasticism. This conjecture is troubling, as clearly Hamlet is the hero of this drama; the 'sweet prince' (5.2.353) who is loved by his people and mourned by Fortinbras. Furthermore, Hamlet is obviously superior to his abjectly non-charismatic uncle, who literally kills his brother like a snake, revives the aforementioned tradition and engages in diplomacy rather than warfare. Indeed, we may even concur with Bloom that Hamlet 'vies with King David and the Jesus of Mark as a charismatic-of-charismatics'.[42] Weber makes three observations about charisma that are prescient when considering the charismatic status of Hamlet: first, charisma is non-economic; second, charisma is non-inheritable, and third, charismatic innovation tends to be absorbed into the existing bureaucratic structure and thus rendered non-charismatic. According to Weber:

> Every charisma is on the road from a turbulently emotional life that knows no economic rationality to a slow death by suffocation under the weight of material interests: every hour of its existence brings it nearer to this end.[43]

This process of suffocation has begun long before we first see Hamlet on the stage, dressed in black and wishing that this 'too too solid flesh would melt' (1.2.129) and that God 'had not fix'd / His canon 'gainst self-slaughter' (1.2.131–132). Hamlet is *not* like his father, yet while he has not inherited his father's warrior status, he has enjoyed a distinct emotional life as a Wittenberg scholar. This emotional life ended when Hamlet returned to Elsinore, long before the play began, and is over before he agrees to his mother's request to forsake his studies and before he renounces scholasticism in order to avenge his father. This life is recalled wistfully by Hamlet during his interaction with the troupe of actors, prompting the aforementioned fit of self-loathing, and the tragedy of *Hamlet* might therefore be described as the slow and painful absorption of the charismatic hero into the bureaucratic and paternalistic regulation of Elsinore.

Hamlet's struggle with the "Danish regulators" might be said to be akin to the imagined plight of the neoliberal hero, who must likewise defy oppressive state machinery to seek his or her autonomy, and indeed the celebration of the "dare and do" of the entrepreneur is one of most distinctive features of the neoliberal canon. For example, in *Anarchy, State and Utopia*, published in 1974, Robert Nozick argues that entrepreneurs identify and respond to opportunities in the market that others have failed to notice, and are *entitled* to the profit thereby accrued because this additional value has been 'created' by their ingenuity.[44] In *Power and Market*, published in 1970, Murray N. Rothbard celebrates the social contribution of the entrepreneur: confronting head-on some of the main objections to the free market, Rothbard argues that the problem of security is answered, in part, by the willingness of the capitalist-entrepreneur to 'assume the bulk of the risks of the market and concomitantly relieve laborers of a great deal of risk'.[45] The libertarian exponent of anarcho-capitalism, Ludwig von Mises, makes a distinction between the entrepreneur and the genius that draws attention to the ubiquity of the former. In *Human Action*, published in 1949, Mises argues that in economics, entrepreneurialism is 'not the particular feature of a special group or class of men; it is inherent in every action and burdens every actor'.[46] In his last book, *The Ultimate Foundation of Economic Science*, published in 1962, Mises claims that the 'feat of the genius is outside the regular flow of human affairs'.[47] Under this argument, gifted individuals operate, like Weber's charismatic, outside the sphere of everyday needs and wants, while the entrepreneur is firmly rooted within this sphere, enhancing it for herself and others. 'If Dante, Shakespeare or Beethoven had died in childhood', he says, 'mankind would miss what it owes them',[48] yet the lingering impression conveyed by Mises is that this loss would be wholly unconscious: it is the *entrepreneur*, rather than the genius, who is the vital everyman of the free market.

Over the centuries, audiences have observed what Samuel Coleridge describes as Hamlet's 'aversion to action',[49] making Hamlet an unlikely template for the neoliberal entrepreneur, and indeed the character in *Hamlet* who corresponds most closely to the neoliberals' model of the "universal" entrepreneur is Hamlet's uncle, who embraces risk and thereby wins what he lasciviously describes as, 'My crown, mine own ambition, and my queen' (3.3.55). In pragmatic terms, the fact that Hamlet's uncle is not charismatic is irrelevant, as this trait is superfluous to his purpose. If Weber is correct, charisma satisfies extraordinary needs, and there is nothing more ordinary than sibling rivalry and lust: "needs" that are most fully satisfied by Machiavellian guile (*see Chapter 3*). Nevertheless, Hamlet's capacity for risk-taking is sufficiently suppressed by the regulation of Elsinore to render him a tragic hero for supporters of neoliberalism.

The permissive society

At the start of this chapter, Education Secretary Keith Joseph's disdain for the "permissive society" was noted. If by permissive we mean the kind of anarchic cruelty demonstrated by Hamlet, then we all might agree with Joseph that education should be anti-permissive. Right-wing economists and philosophers, however, identified a far broader spectrum of deviance in their critique of the permissive society that includes left-wing resistance to paternalistic and bureaucratic structures. In so doing, conservatives seemed to imply that only a *specific* form of defiance is heroic. For example, in his retrospective of Britain in the 1960s, Bernard Levin condemned the abandonment of rationality in the quest for certainty, lamenting that during the sixties 'Talismans, charms, amulets and runic stones with wondrous powers abounded'.[50] This mystical quest was prompted, Levin claims, by a loss of faith in traditional sources of conviction: 'Orthodox religion would not do; authority – political, moral, parental, pedagogical – would not do'.[51] Consequently, health fads, gurus, promiscuity, drug taking and cultural relativism seemed to be the order of the day: in the words of Levin, 'Nothing was sacred'[52] and there was 'Panic and emptiness! Panic and emptiness!'[53] Levin's disgust over this apparent decline in prudence was shared by Buchanan and Rand. With characteristic verve, Rand identified a structural cause for the abandonment of reason, proclaiming that 'The products of America's anti-rational, anti-cognitive "Progressive" education, the hippies, are reverting to the music and the drumbeat of the jungle'.[54] Buchanan was more measured in his appraisal, arguing that young people in the early 1970s did not value order as much as previous generations, and that to their minds the legal structure appeared repressive, as it embodied 'an excess of order relative to liberty of persons'.[55] It is immediately apparent that these two positions mirror Rand and Buchanan's respective stance on rationality: the permissive society is one in which wisdom, for whatever reason, has been forsaken.

In his analysis of the 1960s, Gerard DeGroot appears frustrated by the naiveté of the hippies, who thought that it might be possible to escape the drudgery of alienated work and inhabit a 'storybook world'[56] outside the capitalist system. However, in spite of DeGroot's observation that the directive to 'Turn on, tune in, drop out'[57] was hazardous to many Western teenagers, who ran away from home in pursuit of nirvana and found instead only squalor and drug dependency, the rejection of life in our mechanistic culture is not easily dismissed as irrational.[58] Indeed, the idea that the West was undergoing a cultural decline was viewed as an undeniable truth by many on both the Left and Right of the political spectrum. For example, in *Dialectic of Enlightenment*, published in 1947, Theodor Adorno and Max Horkheimer argued that the mechanism of industrialised labour had been replicated in the amusements offered under late capitalism.[59] We are, they claimed, bombarded by advertisements as we walk down a street, read a newspaper or visit the cinema, and our free time is thus a 'prolongation of work'[60] as we frantically attempt to model our lives according to the dictates of capitalist manufacturers. In the 1950s, Guy Debord encouraged resistance to the machine society, envisioning a 'battle of leisure' between members of the Situationist International who aimed to 'multiply poetic subjects and objects' and the culture industry, with its 'televised imbecilities' that prevent the development of 'political consciousness'.[61] Rand was likewise contemptuous of cultural imbecilities, which she saw as endemic in American society, but she identified a political, rather than economic, reason for their existence. In her novel, *The Fountainhead*, published in 1943, Rand implies that the "dumbing down" of culture is a left-wing conspiracy to undermine our capacity for reason and, by extension, our humanity.[62] According to Rand, the forces of totalitarianism seek to homogenise individuals by robbing us of our ability to perceive anything that transcends the mundane and denying our ability to be transcendent. No longer able to hear 'thunder',[63] she says, we inhabit a diminished world where individuals seek 'mindless "kicks"' in order to 'find a moment's relief from their chronic state of terror'.[64] For right-wing thinkers such as Rand, the enemy was not the corporation selling products to enhance individuals' subjectivity, but the ideologue preaching an anti-individualistic doctrine of fraternity underpinned by universal banality. According to this perspective, the hippies could not possibly find freedom through the adoption of anti-capitalist forms of exchange, as the very notion of the permissive society is a totalitarian trap. Thus, in spite of their diverse views on the limits of rationality, Rand, Buchanan and Hayek shared the conviction that salvation from alienation and dysfunctionality lay not in the rejection of capitalist economic structures, but in the exercise of free choice in the free market.

US conservative and media personality, William F. Buckley, was sufficiently perturbed by the countercultural movement to form a right-wing students' group, Young Americans for Freedom.[65] Drafted in 1960, the YAF's charter proclaimed that 'In time of moral and political crises, it is the responsibility of the youth of America to affirm certain moral truths . . . political freedom cannot long exist without economic freedom'.[66] US economist Milton Friedman echoed this sentiment in *Capitalism and Freedom*, published in 1962, declaring that 'the intellectual descendants of the Philosophical Radicals', including Hayek, were placing their emphasis on 'economic freedom as a means towards political freedom'.[67] Rand attracted her own coterie of student admirers, who formed Ayn Rand clubs and invited her to visit college campuses, and Jennifer Burns reports that in 1965, Rand turned down more than twenty such requests to lecture at colleges and universities.[68] The idea of the Randian hero proved irresistible to many students, who were easily persuaded that laissez-faire capitalism, rather than the hippies' pre-industrial paradise, was the "lost cause" that must be revived. However, while Rand's novels and persona were highly engaging, there is probably some truth in DeGroot's assertion that students adopted pro-market sentiments as an act of rebellion against their more moderate parents. This was, though, no mere flirtation with neoliberalism: DeGroot cautions against conceptualising the 1960s simply as an era of permissiveness, as during this decade the architects of the neoliberal future were being schooled in market ideology, away from the media spotlight. 'By paying so much attention to what was happening on Maggie's Farm', he says, 'we failed to notice the emergence of Maggie Thatcher'.[69]

The change in zeitgeist was slow but certain, and by the 1980s, the idea that young people might "drop out" of capitalism to escape the suffocation of paternalistic and bureaucratic structures was considered passé: instead, they were encouraged to conceptualise the capitalist entrepreneur, rather than the anti-capitalist hippy, as the charismatic revolutionary. Business guru John Kao went so far as to argue that 'the rebel or the truth seeker of the 1960s' had become the 'the entrepreneur of the 1980s'.[70] Harvard duly sponsored its first conference on entrepreneurialism in 1983 in order to discuss how entrepreneurialism might be researched and taught, and certain 'Deweyan themes'[71] (*see Chapter 2*) were married to the neoliberal fascination with market forces to produce enterprise education. According to David Harvey, one of Prime Minister Margaret Thatcher's 'strong ideas'[72] was to forge an alliance between businesses and state actors, and UK state schools were duly encouraged to form links with businesses in order for pupils to gain hands-on experience of the free market economy. In the USA, Michael Apple identified a similar ethos, noting that work experience programmes had been established across the states to help educators 'teach for the needs of industry'.[73]

The wish to bear risk

The belief that the entrepreneurial "wish to bear risk" is fundamentally heroic informs neoliberal economic theory, which states that business managers exercise choice in order to maximise utility (growth; stability; profit) for selfish reasons (personal wealth; power).[74] It is advantageous, therefore, to be a business leader rather than an employee in the free market, as only the self-interest of a CEO is aligned with decision-making, and asymmetric power structures are justified on the grounds that the entrepreneur is willing to bear risk on behalf of herself and others. To reward and encourage individual risk, successive neoliberal governments have passed laws that favour the interests of business leaders and penalise workers by deregulating commerce, weakening the trade unions and lowering the taxes of the super-rich.[75] It has become commonplace for large firms to acquire smaller businesses through hostile takeovers and to then asset-strip those companies, leaving staff demoralised or redundant,[76] yet the entrepreneur's pursuit of self-interest is admired, rather than vilified, by government. For example in the 1990s, UK Trade and Industry Secretary Peter Mandelson proclaimed that, 'We want a society that celebrates and values its business heroes as much as it does its pop stars and footballers'.[77] Economists have provided a moral argument to justify the wealth and status enjoyed by these 'business heroes'. For example, Nozick argues that in a socialist society, there is no way to '*divest* oneself'[78] of the risks of the enterprise one works in, and it is therefore churlish to complain about the wealth enjoyed in capitalist societies by the entrepreneurs who carry this risk on our behalf. According to the precepts of neoliberalism, no one is given "special favour", as the wages for different activities are simply the outcome of the *impersonal* market forces of supply and demand, and according to the marginal productivity theory of income distribution, 'you're worth what you can get'.[79] Presumably, we are all equally free to become the next business hero or popstar in the capitalist state.

Celebration of the pursuit of self-interest has entered education via the discourse of meritocracy, which states that in a free market, individuals may choose to gain a competitive advantage over one another through the accruement of credentials. Allegedly, in a meritocracy we are all free to make the most of our talents, and individuals who use their credentials to gain entry to elite universities, such as Cambridge and Harvard, and the top professions, such as investment banking and corporate law, deserve to live in 'gratuitous affluence'.[80] When stressing the relationship between education and "getting what you are worth", politicians have tended to conflate the willingness to bear risk with the "rational" acceptance of non-charismatic regulation, and to position what Weber describes as 'individually differentiated conduct'[81] as non-entrepreneurial and therefore dysfunctional. Consider, for example, the warning issued by UK Prime Minister Tony Blair:

> Show me an educated youngster and I see someone with great prospects; show me school leavers with no qualifications – who still, deplorably, account for nearly one in ten of 16-year-olds – and I see lives of constant struggle and insecurity.[82]

W. Norton Grubb and Marvin Lazerson note that in many countries including the USA and the UK, students have responded to such warnings by adopting what they describe as a 'highly utilitarian and credentialist' outlook:[83] utilitarian in that they view education solely as a means to future employment, and credentialist in that they focus on 'accumulating the credentials they think necessary, rather than the learning that credentials are supposed to represent'.[84] This obsession with credentials has prompted schools to focus on ends (credentials) rather than means (the development of understanding). In the words of Philip Brown, 'We are creating hordes of smart conformists. They know what they have to do to get ahead, but they have little understanding of why they do what they are doing.'[85] In 2008, the problem of "teaching to the test" was officially recognised by a UK House of Commons Select Committee, which found that a 'variety of classroom practices aimed at improving test results had distorted the education of some children',[86] and that teachers in both primary and secondary schools were impairing pupils' understanding and enjoyment of subjects by focussing on routine exercises and exam preparation. James Ryan has identified a similar problem in the USA, where American teachers have responded to the pressure to raise test scores by teaching the knowledge and skills that will be tested, and 'ignoring more complex aspects of subjects, and some subjects altogether'.[87]

Under neoliberalism, governments are encouraged to take market friendly action to ameliorate market imperfections,[88] and education policy has therefore become a major focus of activity for politicians who would like to ensure maximum employment and national prosperity, but are prohibited from making direct interventions in the economy by the precepts of neoliberalism. In the words of UK Prime Minister Tony Blair, education is 'the best economic policy we have'.[89] In theory, neoliberalism liberates the individual from collective responsibility for risk and cultivates entrepreneurial self-actualisation. In practice, argues Brown, it has led to the emergence of a 'zero-sum game' of employability,[90] in which the winners take most, if not all, of the opportunities available in the free market. Instead of consoling the "losers" in this game, politicians have tended to heighten the perception of individual risk. For example, the ex-head of the CBI and former New Labour minister, Lord Digby Jones, is reported to have claimed that the government should 'starve the jobless back to work' and that anyone who refuses three job offers should be forced to 'live in a hostel on subsistence rations'.[91] Understandably, such rhetoric has stoked parents' fears over their children's pursuit of credentials, and in 2010 the UK relationships counselling body, Relate, announced that it was offering guidance to families on how to cope with stress over their children's GCSEs, A levels and university finals.[92]

The "mitigation of risk" through education is the expression of a much wider economic strategy that places nation states under a similar level of stress to that experienced by individual scholars. As in all market systems, educational interventions to support the economy are dependent upon information about imperfections in the school system, and the gathering of such data has been facilitated by the Organisation for Economic Co-operation and Development (OECD), a US-backed multilateral agency which, along with the World Bank and the International Monetary Fund, has promoted neoliberal ideology across the world.[93] In 2000, the OECD's first Program for International Student Assessment (PISA) report was administered.[94] The PISA is an international assessment that measures 15-year-old students' functional skills in reading, mathematics and science, and this measurement and comparison is justified on the grounds that citizens' functional skills have a direct bearing on national economies. For example, in 2011 the OECD reported that 'the link between education and productivity is very strong' and that 'one extra year of average education leads to an average increase in steady-state long term output per capita by about 4 to 7%'.[95] Entrepreneurial risk is, then, carried by the individual, and national prosperity is an aggregate of individuals' success in the zero-sum game identified by Brown, making investment in education a top priority for governments desperate to cultivate the "right" players in this game.

By identifying pupils as components of an economic system, the OECD locates them in the same paternalistic and bureaucratic structure that Weber identifies as antithetical to charisma. Indeed, the OECD's methodology is highly reminiscent of the measurement process critiqued by Weber in the 1920s. According to Weber:

> With the help of suitable methods of measurement, the optimum profitability of the individual worker is calculated like that of any material of production. On this basis, the American system of "scientific management" triumphantly proceeds with its rational conditioning and training of work performances . . . discipline inexorably takes over ever larger areas as the satisfaction of political and economic needs is increasingly rationalized. This universal phenomenon more and more restricts the importance of charisma and of individually differentiated conduct.[96]

Action that 'restricts the importance of charisma and of individually differentiated conduct' seems to be incompatible with the neoliberal conception of the heroic entrepreneur, yet neoliberal education policy appears to be designed with this restriction in mind. This contradiction was perhaps inevitable, as by seeking to identify entrepreneurialism as a universal expression of rationality that supports the day-to-day function of the economy, economists such as Mises have rendered entrepreneurialism non-charismatic, and have positioned the entrepreneur as yet another "regulator" in a system that seeks to nullify charismatic opposition and creative revolution. Robert Peston has expressed concern over the hedge-fund and private equity 'brain drain' of talented young people who have opted for careers in finance in preference to more socially useful and creative endeavours,[97] presumably because they subscribe to the belief that "You are worth what you can get", rather than the belief that "Some things are worth doing". What is perhaps of greater concern is the tacit assumption, expressed by politicians such as Mandelson, that we should *admire* regulators, whose authority is derived from their position in a system that oppresses dissent.

Conclusion

In the 1970s, Nozick called for a 'minimal state' that recognises our rights and allows us 'to choose our life and to realize our ends and our conception of ourselves, insofar as we can, aided by the voluntary cooperation of other individuals possessing the same dignity'.[98] Instead of achieving this neoliberal utopia, we have, it seems, come closer to the totalitarian model reviled by writers such as Rand. As James Marshall puts it:

> . . . the demands of performativity mean not the pursuit of educational ideals, like personal autonomy, or emancipation but, instead, the subsumption of education under the demands of efficiency for the total social system.[99]

To understand why neoliberalism has failed in this manner we need look no further than the arguments against the permissive society outlined earlier in this chapter. The "irrationality" of the countercultural movement was, ultimately, intolerable to many exponents of laissez-faire capitalism, who, in spite of their diverse opinions on the limits of rationality, set great store by the exercise of reason in the free market. Consequently, the idea of self-actualisation through the expression of free choice in the market society has become so closely aligned in the neoliberal imagination with rational calculation that the scope for the expression of charismatic imaginative play has been severely curtailed. In spite of neoliberal policy makers' professed fascination with the heroic individual, neoliberalism is delivering to students across the world the emotional life not of Hamlet the charismatic scholar, but of Elsinore, the total social system.

Notes

1 Denham, A. & Garnett, M. (2001) *Keith Joseph*. Chesham: Acumen Publishing Limited. p. xi.
2 Ibid.
3 Ibid: 9.
4 Ibid: 262.
5 Rossiter, A.P. (1961: 187) *Angel with Horns and Other Shakespeare Lectures*. New York: Theatre Arts Books.
6 Greenblatt, S. (1997: 1661) 'Introduction to *Hamlet*' In: *The Norton Shakespeare*. New York, NY: W.W. Norton & Company, Inc. pp. 1659–1667.
7 Ibid: 1661.
8 Ibid.
9 Holbrook, P. (2010) *Shakespeare's Individualism*. Cambridge: Cambridge University Press.
10 Ibid: 77.
11 Rand, A. (1975) *The Romantic Manifesto*. Second Revised Edition. London: Signet, Penguin Books Ltd.
12 Holbrook (2010: 13).
13 Rand (1964) *The Virtue of Selfishness*. New York: Signet. p. 28.
14 Ibid: 28–29. Italics in original.
15 Bloom, H. (1999) *Shakespeare: The Invention of the Human*. London: Fourth Estate. p. 385.
16 Ibid: 404.
17 Rand, A. (2007) *Atlas Shrugged*. London: Penguin Books Ltd. p. 1012. Italics in original.
18 Ibid. Italics in original.
19 Rand (1964).

20 Burns, J. (2011) *Goddess of the Market: Ayn Rand and the American Right*. Oxford: Oxford University Press.
21 Shuggart II, W.F. (2008) *The Concise Encyclopaedia of Economics: Public Choice*. Available online at: http://www.econlib.org/library/Enc/PublicChoice.html [Accessed 23rd September 2015].
22 Buchanan, J.M. (2000) *The Limits of Liberty: Between Anarchy and Leviathan*. Indianapolis: Liberty Fund Inc. p. 3.
23 Ibid: 12.
24 Rand (1964).
25 Buchanan (2000: 212).
26 Ibid.
27 Hayek, F.A. (2011) *The Constitution of Liberty: The Definitive Edition*. Hamowy, R. (ed.). Chicago: The University of Chicago Press.
28 Ibid: 112.
29 Ibid: 120.
30 Ibid.
31 Ibid: 128.
32 Ibid: 108.
33 Ibid: 128.
34 Horwitz, S. (2005) 'Two Worlds at Once: Rand, Hayek and the Ethics of Micro- and Macro-cosmos' *The Journal of Ayn Rand Studies*, 6 (2), pp. 375–403.
35 Ibid.
36 Buchanan (2000: 211).
37 Weber, M. (1978) *Economy and Society: An Outline of Interpretive Sociology*. London: University of California Press, Ltd.
38 Ibid: 1111.
39 Ibid: 1117.
40 Ibid.
41 Ibid.
42 Bloom (1999: 384).
43 Weber (1978: 1120).
44 Nozick, R. (1974) *Anarchy, State, and Utopia*. New York: Basic Books.
45 Rothbard, M. (2004) *Man, Economy and State: A Treatise on Economic Principles with Power and Market: Government and the Economy*. Auburn, AL: The Ludwig von Mises Institute. p. 1313.
46 Mises, L.v. (1966) *Human Action: A Treatise on Economics*. Third Revised Edition. Chicago: Henry Regnery Company. pp. 252–253.
47 Mises, L.v. (1978) *The Ultimate Foundation of Economic Science: An Essay on Method*. Second Edition. Kansas City: Sheed Andrews and McNeel, Inc. p. 61.
48 Ibid.
49 Coleridge, S. (1827/1969: 178) 'Hamlet' In: Hawkes, T. (ed.) *Coleridge on Shakespeare*. Harmondsworth: Penguin Books Ltd. pp. 157–185.
50 Levin, B. (1970) *The Pendulum Years: Britain and the Sixties*. London: Pan Books Ltd. p. 30.
51 Ibid.
52 Ibid: 324.
53 Ibid: 314.
54 Rand (1975: 54).
55 Buchanan (2011: 162).
56 DeGroot, G. (2008) *The 60s Unplugged: A Kaleidoscopic History of a Disorderly Decade*. London: Macmillan. p. 249.
57 Ibid: 209.
58 Adorno, T.W. & Horkheimer, M. (1997) *Dialectic of Enlightenment*. Cumming, J. (trans.) London: Verso.

59 Ibid.
60 Ibid: 137.
61 Debord, G. (2003: 703) 'Writings from the Situationist International' In: Harrison, C. & Wood, P. (eds.) *Art in Theory 1900–2000*. Oxford: Blackwell. pp. 701–707.
62 Rand, A. (2007) *The Fountainhead*. London: Penguin Books Ltd.
63 Ibid: 489.
64 Rand (1964: 31).
65 DeGroot (2008: 244).
66 YAF in DeGroot (2008: 244).
67 Friedman, M. (2002) *Capitalism and Freedom*. Chicago: The University of Chicago Press. p. 11.
68 Burns (2011).
69 DeGroot (2008: 450).
70 Kao, J. in Ward, S.C. (2013: 114) 'Creativity, Freedom and the Crash: How the Concept of Creativity was Used as a Bulwark against Communism during the Cold War, and as a Means to Reconcile Individuals to Neoliberalism Prior to the Great Recession' *Journal for Critical Education Policy Studies*, *11* (3), pp. 110–126.
71 Fairfield, P. (2009) *Education after Dewey*. London: Continuum International Publishing Group.
72 Harvey, D. (2009) *A Brief History of Neoliberalism*. Oxford: Oxford University Press. p. 76.
73 Apple, M. (1995) *Education and Power*. Second Edition. London: Routledge. p. 126.
74 Hill, R. & Myatt, T. (2010) *The Economics Anti-textbook: A Critical Thinker's Guide to Microeconomics*. London: Zed Books.
75 Harvey (2009).
76 Peston, R. (2008) *Who Runs Britain?* London: Hodder & Stoughton Ltd.
77 Mandelson, P. (1998) 'The Ever-Louder Tick: Blair's Britain and the Debt Timebomb' In: Elliot, L. & Atkinson, D. (ed.) (2007) *Fantasy Island: Waking up to the Incredible Economic, Political and Social Illusions of the Blair Legacy*. London: Constable & Robinson Ltd. p. 47.
78 Nozick (1974: 256) Italics in original.
79 Hill & Myatt (2010: 169).
80 Brown, P. (2006: 395) 'The Opportunity Trap' In: Lauder, H., Brown, P., Dillabough, J.-A. & Halsey, A.H. (eds.) *Education, Globalization & Social Change*. Oxford: Oxford University Press. pp. 381–397.
81 Weber (1978: 1156).
82 Blair, T. (1998) *The Third Way: New Politics for the New Century*. London: The Fabian Society. p. 10.
83 Grubb, W.N. & Laverson, M. (2006: 301) 'The Globalization of Rhetoric and Practice: The Education Gospel and Vocationalism' In: Lauder, H., Brown, P., Dillabough, J.-A. & Halsey, A.H. (eds.) *Education, Globalization & Social Change*. Oxford: Oxford University Press. pp. 295–307.
84 Ibid.
85 Brown (2006: 393).
86 The Children, Schools and Families Committee (2008) *Testing and Assessment*. London: The Stationery Office Limited. p. 3.
87 Ryan, J. (2012) *Struggling for Inclusion: Educational Leadership in a Neoliberal World*. Charlotte, NC: Information Age Publishing, Inc. p. 32.
88 Lapavitsas, S. (2005) 'Mainstream Economics in the Neoliberal Era' In: Saad-Filho, A. & Johnson, D. (eds.) *Neoliberalism: A Critical Reader* (30–40). London: Pluto Press. p. 37.
89 Blair, T. in Barber, M. (1997) *The Learning Game*. London: Indigo. p. 46.
90 Brown (2006: 394).

91 Jones, D. cited in Seymour, R. (2010) *The Meaning of David Cameron*. Ropley: O-Books. pp. 59–60.

92 Asthana, A. (2010) 'Parents Offered Counselling over Exam Tensions' *The Observer* 30th May 2010, p. 6.

93 Connolly, R. (2013) 'Have You Ever Considered a Career in Total Revolution? Drama and the Corporate Reform of Higher Education' *Studies in Theatre and Performance, 33* (2), pp. 225–243.

94 NCES (2013) Program for International Student Assessment (PISA). Available online at: http://nces.ed.gov/surveys/pisa/ [Accessed 28th November 2013].

95 Gurria, A. (2011) *Skills for the 21 Century: From Lifetime Employment to Lifetime Employability*. Remarks by Angel Gurría, OECD Secretary-General, delivered at the Joint Vienna Institute. Available online at: http://www.oecd.org/employment/skillsforthe21centuryfromlifetimeemploymenttolifetimeemployability.htm [Accessed 27th November 2015]

96 Weber (1978: 1156).

97 Peston, R. (2008) *Who Runs Britain?* London: Hodder & Stoughton Ltd. p. 193.

98 Nozick (1974: 334).

99 Marshall, J.D. (1999: 310) 'Performativity: Lyotard and Foucault through Searle and Austin' *Studies in Philosophy and Education*, 18, pp. 309–317.

2   Performativity

Measure for Measure

Introduction

In 2013, Stephen Ball and Antonio Olmedo[1] published excerpts from email correspondence with educators in the UK and USA in despair over the political constraints placed on their practice, and in particular the use of school inspections to condition their self-conceptualisation as teachers. In the words of one school principal, 'To think differently – that is to engage in learning rather than pseudo-measuring – is to be subjected to a totalitarian human and public relations meltdown'.[2] Ball has written extensively about the intrusion of performance measures in education, claiming that 'the data-base, the appraisal meeting, the annual review, report writing, the regular publication of results and promotion applications, inspections and peer reviews'[3] constitute the 'terror of performativity'.[4] Ball defines performativity as a set of disciplines that requires us 'to spend increasing amounts of our time in making ourselves accountable, reporting on what we do rather than doing it',[5] and claims that the terror of performativity is directed inwards by teachers who are encouraged to blame themselves for failing to meet externally imposed standards for teaching. This preoccupation with 'reporting on what we do'[6] has, according to Ball, rendered teachers 'transparent but empty'.[7] In the previous chapter, I explored the neoliberals' rejection of the "irrationality" of the permissive society and alluded to their dismissal of progressivism as an adjunct to the collectivism favoured by anti-capitalists. Michael Apple argues that neoliberal ideology has led us to believe that Public is bad and Private is good,[8] and while this prejudice stems from the belief that the sharing of risk in collectivist societies is anti-heroic, the relationship between this ideology and the practice of performativity is less obvious. To illuminate what Ball describes as the 'struggle for the teacher's soul'[9] inherent to the neoliberal project, and to consider in particular what performativity aims to 'empty' out of the teaching profession, in this chapter I offer a reading of Shakespeare's *Measure for Measure*. Described as a 'problem play'[10] due to its complex and at times baffling juxtaposition of dark and comic elements, *Measure for Measure* is considered so impenetrable that critics have variously dismissed it as nonsense and hailed it as a magnificent poem, rather than a conventional stage play.[11] Shakespeare's subtle depiction of clandestine knowledge as a means to influence action has prompted

Jonathan Dollimore[12] to describe *Measure for Measure* as a drama of *surveillance*, making it a highly appropriate lens through which to scrutinise the terror of performativity.

Measure for Measure

The dramatic premise of *Measure for Measure* is simple: the law against fornication is being ignored in Vienna. From this simple starting point a succession of perplexing events unfolds. Rather than risk damaging his public image by enforcing the law against fornication, the Duke of Vienna feigns the need for overseas travel and appoints Angelo his deputy. Believing Angelo to be of a vigorous moral disposition, the Duke is confident that he will awaken the dormant penalties against licentiousness. However, rather than simply leave Angelo to get on with this task, the Duke puts on the disguise of a friar to covertly observe events, and a pantomime of calamities ensues centred on Angelo's desire to zealously enforce the law whilst covertly breaking it. The peculiarities of governance in Vienna thus form the basis of comedy in *Measure for Measure*, and Shakespeare's interest in this topic is arguably the expression of what Michel Foucault identifies as the Renaissance fascination with governance.[13] According to Foucault's analysis, *Measure for Measure* was written at a point of rupture with what he describes as the medieval, theocratic, 'pastoral' modality of power.[14] Foucault describes how, in the wake of the publication of Niccolò Machiavelli's sixteenth-century treatise on governance, *The Prince* (*see Chapter 3*), the idea began to form that the art of government must find its doctrines of rationality in state business, rather than seeking them in 'transcendental rules, a cosmological model, or a philosophico-moral ideal'.[15] Otto von Gierke describes the situation pithily: 'The state was no longer derived from the Divinely ordained harmony of the universal whole . . . it was simply explained by itself'.[16] This new modality of power retained the medieval 'pastoral' interest in knowing the contents of people's minds, but shifted its focus from general humanity to the amalgamation of individuals who constitute the state.[17]

In *Measure for Measure*, the pastoral and secular modalities of power are explored through Shakespeare's depiction of the Duke and his deputy, Angelo. Given authority over the subjects of Vienna, Angelo personifies earthly law and thus attempts to direct individuals' behaviour by appealing to their faculty for reason, rather than their religious beliefs. Angelo's attempts to direct reason are an amusing flop, particularly with regard to his encounter with Pompey the pimp, who in soliloquy reveals his determination not to allow his ideals to be thrashed out of him, even though the threat of violence and the offer of a lucrative post have jointly persuaded him of the logic of relinquishing his profession. As Pompey puts it, 'The valiant heart's not whipt out of his trade' (2.1.253), and Angelo's "reform" of Pompey thus amounts to his rational and self-interested exchange of illegal for legal behaviour with no alteration to his conscience. Pompey's heart may indeed remain in his former trade while his body complies with the law.

According to Richard Hooker, Shakespeare's contemporaries believed that state law had power over 'outward actions only'[18] and that *religion* worked upon individuals' 'inward cognitions',[19] and in light of Hooker's analysis we might expect the Duke to enjoy greater success than Angelo when he assumes the disguise of a friar, as the symbol of spiritual law, and sets about becoming the "conscience" of Vienna. The disguised Duke's first experiment is upon Claudio's pregnant lover, Juliet, to whom he declares, 'I'll teach you how you shall arraign your conscience' (2.3.21). Juliet readily submits to the Duke's feigned spiritual authority, but towards the end of the play this ability to instruct souls deserts the Duke entirely when he encounters the condemned prisoner, Barnardine. The disguised Duke tells the drunken Barnardine, 'Sir, induc'd by my charity, and hearing how / hastily you are to depart, I am come to advise you, / comfort you, and pray with you' (4.3.49–51). This 'charity' does not impress Barnardine, who cuts off the Duke's intercession with his own command, 'Not a word' (4.3.61). It seems, then, that the disguised Duke's ability to transform his subjects' 'inward cognitions' is dependent upon their willingness to accept his spiritual counsel, making irreligious characters such as Barnardine impossible to work upon.

Through his depiction of the different modalities of power deployed by the Duke and Angelo, Shakespeare seems to imply that the human mind is somewhat resistant to injunctions of faith and reason alike; a phenomenon Peter Holbrook attributes to Shakespeare's love of individual freedom,[20] which he claims is expressed through characters who refuse to allow their minds to be bent by interfering missionaries such as the Duke or imperious bullies like Angelo. At the conclusion of the drama we are invited to celebrate the reprieve of individuals who are guilty of fornication and duplicity. This apparent failure of the Duke to uphold the law against fornication has led some critics to condemn *Measure for Measure* as 'unwholesome, cynical or morally equivocal'.[21] Yet, in spite of Samuel Coleridge's assertion that *Measure for Measure* is a 'hateful work' that grossly wounds our feelings of justice,[22] it is difficult to imagine a happy resolution to this strange story that is *not* morally equivocal.

Neoliberal governance

The elections of Prime Minister Thatcher in 1979 and President Reagan in 1980 marked the beginning of the formal dominance of neoliberal policy in the UK and USA, and the "permissive society" and its educational manifestations were duly targeted for eradication. Arguably, this eradication resembled the Duke and Angelo's corporeal and spiritual crackdown on fornication. The use of what Foucault identifies as the reason-based modality of power in this mission was immediately apparent: President Reagan's 1983 report, A Nation at Risk, stimulated rational debate about accountability by identifying alleged weakness in the US education system,[23] and in 2002, President George W. Bush signed the No Child Left Behind act into law, enabling teacher efficacy to be assessed through the high-stakes testing of pupils. Since then many states have chosen to implement a high-stakes teacher evaluation (HSTE) system as a seemingly logical response to school failure.[24] Similarly, in 1988, the UK's Education Reform Act established political control over the curriculum and created a quasi-market by mandating the publication of schools' assessment results and giving parents the freedom to employ their capacity for rational choice to 'vote with their children's feet'.[25]

In addition to the identification of schools' performance in league tables, politicians also wielded the medieval theocentric modality of power to discern and guide the consciences of individual teachers. In 1992, the UK government enhanced its ability to monitor teaching and the delivery of the National Curriculum through The Education Schools Act, which transformed the nature of school inspection in the UK by sweeping aside Her Majesty's Inspectorate (HMI), a small independent body of inspectors which had been established in the early years of Queen Victoria's reign,[26] and replacing it with a new government department, the Office for Standards in Education (OFSTED). UK Prime Minister John Major triumphantly declared ahead of this policy that 'The progressive theorists have had their say, and they have had their day'.[27] In their 1996 study of the emotional impact of an on OFSTED inspection, Bob Jeffrey and Peter Woods found that, far from being inspired to repent of their past ways by OFSTED, the teachers denounced the Registered Inspector as 'inhuman',[28] and protested furiously that they were not 'robots'[29] who would consent to abandon their humanity in order to embrace what they saw as inflexible teaching practice. We might note here the parallel between the description of the Registered Inspector and *Measure for Measure*'s Angelo, whom the Duke describes as a man who 'scare confesses / That his blood flows; or that his appetite / Is more to bread than stone' (1.3.52–53).

Eve Tuck urges us to recognise that neoliberalism 'is concerned with the dispossession and erasure of the unworthy subject'.[30] We might add to this, arguing that the neoliberal project seeks to combine the erasure of progressivism with a particular form of pedagogic self-actualisation and self-regulation through the direction of 'gaze', as theorised by Foucault in his analysis of contemporary state power.[31] According to Foucault, modern-day governance is achieved through a process of internalisation whereby each person becomes his own overseer, simultaneously performing the role of "Angelo the objective rational controller" and "the Duke as subjective spiritual guide", 'exercising this surveillance over, and against, himself'.[32] In her study of the mandatory Professional Growth Plans of teachers in Alberta, Canada, Tara Fenwick argues that through these 'technologies of self-governance',[33] teachers have internalised 'dominant notions of the ideal teaching self as an active, continuous, self-regulating learner'.[34] Although some of the teachers in Fenwick's study appeared to welcome their own surveillance, finding much to admire in log books of professional improvement, elsewhere teachers' reluctance to self-regulate as neoliberal subjects has resulted in the adoption of punitive measures to enforce both theocentric and rational modalities of governance. For example, building on the accountability platform of No Child Left Behind, President Barack Obama's 2009 Race to the Top initiative obliged teachers to align their behaviour with politically determined values by incentivising states to calibrate teacher salaries to student test scores. Timothy Ford et al.'s analysis of *Compass*, a high-stakes teacher evaluation (HSTE) in Louisiana,[35] yields a critique of dehumanisation similar to that proffered by Jeffrey and Woods. According to Ford et al., research on the effects of linking US teacher evaluations to student achievement and firing teachers who 'fail' has revealed 'overall declines in working conditions, including teacher morale, efficacy, and locus of control'.[36] Frustrated perhaps by this loss of control, many of the elementary teachers in Ford et al.'s study questioned the validity of *Compass* as a reflection of their teaching practice, and professed that 'the pursuit of "fun" was a key source of fulfilment in their professional lives'.[37] With all such 'psychic rewards'[38] curtailed by *Compass*, several teachers in the study decided to quit the profession. One third-grade teacher who resigned said, 'I feel like I test the kids constantly to accommodate the needs – not the kids' needs, the "top people's" needs'.[39] Perhaps not surprisingly, Ford et al. report that questions such as 'Should I go work at Walmart?' are commonly articulated by teachers who feel they are 'being bullied' into drilling children for tests.[40] Amongst teachers today there is, it seems, an echo of Pompey's avowal that 'The valiant heart's not whipt out of his trade' (2.1.253), yet the number of teachers leaving the profession is a testament to the difficulty of maintaining this position.

For Holbrook, part of the appeal of Shakespeare is his subversive rejection of constrictive morality, and arguably the oppression of teachers and the silencing of non-neoliberal voices in the discourse of education are manifestations of the same moral constriction critiqued by Shakespeare in *Measure for Measure*. Indeed, in light of *Measure for Measure*, we might question Hayek's theory that the expression of free choice is bound up with individuals' liberty, as this play indicates that if individuals can be persuaded by policy makers to believe, like the pregnant lover Juliet, that they have *chosen* to reject their previous behaviour (as in Fenwick's study), then the bold intransigence displayed by individuals like Barnardine and Pompey may evaporate. In *The Virtue of Selfishness*, published in 1964, Rand presented her own moral code for the free-market society, arguing that we are ethically obliged to avoid the use of fraud or force in our dealings with others,[41] yet this guidance for marketised relations appears to have been disregarded in the domain of education.

It is difficult to see how the manipulation of teachers' choice of behaviour through the terror of performativity will lead to their self-regulation as autonomous beings. We might, therefore, find ourselves asking 'Why is this happening?' A possible explanation for the neoliberal promotion of such "terror" is that it makes teachers embrace entrepreneurial risk alongside their pupils. However, many teachers have been left puzzled over why their previous practice is not deemed to be entrepreneurial, when it afforded them greater pedagogic freedom than they currently enjoy. It is perhaps more likely that the terror of performativity aims to eradicate a pedagogic freedom that has been conflated in the minds of policy makers with the "permissive society". By considering what is deemed to be "permissive" about pre-neoliberal education, we may perhaps go further in understanding the rationale of performativity.

"Permissive" progressivism

In the nineteenth century, philosophers in Germany considered the power of learning to create what Friedrich Froebel termed a 'harmonious personality'[42] – not through children's engagement with their nation's cultural artefacts, but through the promotion of co-operative and mutually helpful living.[43] Froebel's Romantic ideas inspired the American educational philosopher, John Dewey, who from 1896 ran the Chicago experiment in which he educated children age four to fourteen. Dewey's experimental findings led him to conclude that all knowledge is personal and is made by each individual for himself for the purpose of adapting himself to new situations.[44] As such, Dewey's ideas shared some ground with the Renaissance theory of self-actualisation through education. However, while the humanists posited certain texts as key to self-development, Dewey challenged the notion that there exists an absolute truth that can be transmitted to the scholar, since the meaning of a concept depends on its relationship to the individual. For Dewey, personal growth is the product of the individual's Darwinian adaptation to the unfamiliar, and while the result of thought is important to the individual, it is subsidiary to the process of thought,[45] and he therefore rejected the attempt to indoctrinate children with cultural materials that ghettoise human experience. Instead, Dewey promoted democracy as a spirit of enquiry that cultivates individuals' ethical co-operation through shared experience,[46] and in so doing, he positioned progressive education as a means to develop the child's freedom of thought and social connectivity.

Contemporaneously with Dewey's research, the Progressive movement campaigned against the social inequities fostered and sustained by capitalism in the USA,[47] and while this political movement waned in popularity during the 1920s, the progressive educational movement went from strength to strength.[48] De-politicised, progressivism was viewed as a pragmatic method of instruction underpinned by empirical evidence about the importance of play and discovery for children's cognitive development, and its popularity was due, in part, to its perceived status as an 'individualist revolt against Puritan restraint and a celebration of the creative impulses in all individuals.'[49] The historic association between child-centred learning and political Progressivism was, however, never entirely forgotten, and the promotion of Dewey's idea of 'conjoint and cooperative doings'[50] proved controversial in the latter half of the twentieth century. As discussed in Chapter 1, "permissive" anti-capitalist sentiment was dismissed by neoliberals as irrational, and Ayn Rand offered a characteristically distinctive critique of the socialist dimension of progressivism through her rejection of altruism. Rand defines altruism as the ethical principle that 'man has no right to exist for his own sake'[51] as his existence is only justified through his service to others, and that 'self-sacrifice is his highest moral duty, virtue and value'.[52] Shakespeare offers a subtle exploration of altruism in *Measure for Measure* through his depiction of Isabella's ethical dilemma. If Isabella forfeits her virginity, her brother lives; if she maintains her honour, he dies. Of course, the comic premise of *Measure for Measure* would have been difficult to sustain if Isabella had opted for self-sacrifice, but this plotline is not merely expedient: our response to Isabella's choice is tantalisingly indicative of our subjective position on the virtue of self-sacrifice – a sensation that is acutely discomforting for critics such as Coleridge and precludes the play's dismissal as simple farce.

In the twentieth century, uncertainty over whether self-sacrifice should be considered an expression of rational individualism or anti-rational collectivism stemmed, in no small part, from unease over the promotion of 'conjoint and cooperative'[53] activities by the National Socialists under Adolf Hitler. In 1934, a set of Ten Laws for Students was published that commanded the subjugation of the self to the collective, proclaiming for example 'There is no freedom in unrestrained behaviour and a lack of ties'; 'Be a comrade!'.[54] Members of the Hitler Youth were likewise told that 'the Fürher demands of you and of us all that we train ourselves to a life of service and duty, of loyalty and comradeship'.[55] This collectivism was aligned with pedagogic practices that centred on the cultivation of 'folk' identity rather than respect for elite culture.[56] J. Noakes and G. Pridham note that an important aspect of Nazi education was the belief that the cult of 'Experience' (*Erlebnis*) is more important to the development of the individual than the academic process of learning (*Wissenschaft*) with its stress on 'knowledge' (*Erkenntnis*).[57] According to this ideology, the 'deep truths of Nazism' couldn't be accessed through intellectual enquiry as they 'involved 'feeling' (*Gefühl*)' through action.[58] The anti-rational thrust of Nazism found infamous expression through the burning of "un-German" books; an activity that bore, for some critics, an uncomfortable resemblance to the progressive educationalists' rejection of tradition.

According to Lindsay Paterson, a 'common theme'[59] in the left-wing response to fascism during the 1930s was the proclamation of socialism's adherence to reason. For British socialists such as Harold Laski, Paterson claims, 'Fascism was, first of all, simply stupid . . . It was only by destroying proper education that the Nazis could have triumphed'.[60] "Proper" education was held by these socialists to be synonymous with the tradition extolled by Matthew Arnold, the nineteenth-century poet, cultural critic and Her Majesty's Inspector of Schools. Reflecting on the potential for spiritual anarchy in Victorian England, Arnold proposed that social disaster might be averted through the development of national cultural unity.[61] In a variation of Jean-Jacques Rousseau's earlier vision of education as a component of nation building, Arnold suggested that culture might be used to "Hellenise" what he saw as the rapidly expanding, philistine English middle class. Arnold poured scorn on the notion that England's greatness lay in her coal reserves, proclaiming that England's true and enduring wealth was her cultural heritage. Arnold thereby echoed the belief extolled by the Ancient Greek rhetorician Isocrates that the true greatness of Athens resided in its superior culture.[62] Under this model of education, a strong society is dependent upon individuals' access to their culture according to their innate ability. A country that fails to cultivate 'its own best sons'[63] risks being dominated by degenerate demagogues and is no longer worth defending.

Not surprisingly, notes Paterson, British socialists in the pre-war period were somewhat dismissive of progressivism and its rejection of tradition, yet during the "permissive" decade of the1960s something of an intellectual revolution occurred that led to the rehabilitation of *feeling through action*. An obvious objection to the stance adopted by Laski and his fellow intellectuals was that the veneration of elite culture consolidates, rather than challenges, tradition and the material circumstances in which it is located, including social stratification along class lines. Roger Dale describes the 1960s as the Golden Age of progressivism,[64] when the idea of acclimatising children to the needs of the modern capitalist society was rejected anew by members of the countercultural revolution on both sides of the Atlantic. Inspired by Dewey's assertion that democracy and freedom are dependent upon a sense of community and shared purpose, and that schools should be organised as co-operative communities to cultivate this ethos,[65] progressive educators advocated a range of tactics to challenge the status quo. For example, Ivan Illich claimed that traditional education normalises the unequal distribution of power,[66] and the Deschooling movement duly sought to eradicate this inequality by removing institutions that repress individuals (*see Chapter 6*). At the same time, the more gentle 'hippy' movement sought to retreat from social inequity into what Dale describes as an 'idealized pre-industrial rural community' of learners.[67]

The new sociology of education

Although the countercultural movement was dismissed by conservatives as irrational, the intellectual basis for the rejection of tradition was couched in highly rational terminology by exponents of what Michael Young described in 1971 as the New Sociology of Education.[68] Advocates of this new sociology subscribed to the 'SAD thesis' that pupils' life chances are determined by their social advantage or disadvantage,[69] and during the 1970s, left-wing sociologists such as Pierre Bourdieu argued that educators who base curricula on elite culture consolidate the social advantage of children born into the 'habitus'[70] of privilege. Jonathan Rose's analysis of this new ideology reveals the similarity between the left-wing sociologists' rejection of social stratification through the privileging of elite culture in schools and the fascist anti-intellectualism critiqued by socialists in the 1930s. According to Rose, the new sociology of education held that knowledge is socially constructed and that consequently 'the learner is competent to define the content', 'all subcultures are equally valuable' and that 'academic knowledge is not superior to other kinds of knowledge'.[71] The most inflammatory aspect of the new sociology of education was, perhaps, the belief that instead of 'offering all classes the kind of education traditionally enjoyed by the elite, schools should value and preserve folk cultures'.[72] For conservatives, the countercultural movement's anti-intellectual fascination with folksy sentiment bore an uncomfortable resemblance to fascistic altruism.

In the UK, anxiety over the apparent assault on the nation's intellectual tradition by left-wing ideologues was stoked by media coverage of a series of high-profile scandals, such as the William Tynedale Junior School affair of 1974–76, in which head teacher Terry Ellis excited public indignation by running his school as a co-operative, allowing pupils flexibility over what and when they learned, and declaring that he 'did not give a damn about parents'.[73] In the USA, similar concerns over the empowerment of ideologically driven teachers inspired the economist Milton Friedman to unveil his economic solution of consumer control over school choice.[74] UK Prime Minister James Callaghan attempted to allay fears over the collapse of traditional values in education in his Ruskin Speech of 1976, in which he launched the Great Debate about education, questioning the merits of "trendy" teaching methods and advocating an alignment of the curriculum with the needs of industry. At the heart of concern over "trendy" teachers and their unorthodox methods was the belief, slowly but surely growing, that social evil springs not from social division, as postulated by Dewey,[75] but instead from the breakdown of traditional values, and that politicians should focus on the maintenance of these values while leaving the market free to govern itself.[76] Viewed through the neoliberal lens, progressive teachers resembled the citizens of Shakespeare's Vienna: as a consequence of political leniency they had lapsed into a casual disregard for pedagogic propriety and needed to be guided "back to basics".

Neoliberal objections to progressivism

The neoliberal rejection of progressivism has not been absolute. On the practical level, Dewey's claim that experiential knowledge enables the individual to become autonomous chimes with the willingness to bear risk discussed in Chapter 1, and has proved useful to neoliberal politicians wishing to posit material success as the product of individuals' adaptation to their environment. On the philosophical level, certain aspects of progressivism chime with neoliberal sentiment, and Paul Fairfield highlights in particular the political appeal of Dewey's criticism of 'formal analysis', which 'rejects experimental reasoning in favour of a top-down application of technical categories'.[77] Margaret Thatcher famously proclaimed 'There is no such thing as society',[78] and the progressive educationalists' assertion that top-down social categories should be rejected on the grounds that classifying social phenomena into conceptual structures divorces reason from experience[79] thus complements the neoliberals' atomized view of society. On the other hand, Dewey's argument that learning should take the form of a democratic moral enquiry in which children learn how to take part in 'conjoint and cooperative doings'[80] is obviously at odds with neoliberal atomisation. Furthermore, Dewey's criticism of our tendency to naturalise what he saw as the cultural and therefore artificial division between the empirical knowing of the 'trained' working class, who 'are controlled by direct concern with things',[81] and the higher rational knowing of the 'educated' upper class, 'who are free to cultivate themselves'[82] is considered suspect by neoliberals. As discussed in Chapter 1, 'higher rational knowing' is prized by neoliberal philosophers, and we might therefore expect them to take a dim view of any theory that appears to challenge its pre-eminence, as in the example of Rand's contempt for 'jungle' thinking cited in that chapter.

The reassertion of tradition

As we have seen, during the early twentieth century arguments in favour of tradition were closely aligned with socialist ideas about democratic participation; a debate to which Hayek was keen to contribute. In *The Road to Serfdom*, published in 1944, Hayek argued that the law is not something to be meddled with, even in the pursuit of individual liberty, as deviation from tradition may have unforeseen consequences for power relationships.[83] Citing the example of Nazi Germany, Hayek contrasted the Nazis' 'moral state' with the 'liberal state', arguing that in the former the government must 'impose its valuations upon people and, instead of assisting them in advancement of their own ends, choose the ends for them'.[84] In the 'moral state' the law is 'an instrument used by the lawgiver upon the people and for his ends'.[85] Contemplation of Hayek's philosophy reveals the subtlety of *Measure for Measure*, as the Duke both adheres to and deviates from Hayek's recommended course. Consistent with Hayek, the Duke does not favour abandoning law that governs personal morality in the manner of a libertarian, yet his behaviour is also typical of the 'moral state' critiqued by Hayek, as he seeks to revive a law, or tradition, that has been so long neglected that a new mode of living has arisen that is threatened by the Duke's moral mission – a problem most conspicuous in the case of Claudio and his pregnant lover, Juliet.

The difficulty of both determining and maintaining "tradition" has created something of a philosophical conundrum for exponents of neoliberalism: theorists such as Hayek favour the preservation of tradition over moral intervention, yet the defence of traditional values may require moral intervention, which compromises freedom. Arguably, this conundrum is as complex as anything offered for analysis by Shakespeare in *Measure for Measure*. In *The Constitution of Liberty*, published in 1960, Hayek attempted to rebuke the idea that the moral intervention of state education renders it an illiberal or totalitarian activity:

> In contemporary society, the case for compulsory education up to a certain minimum standard is twofold. There is the general argument that all of us will be exposed to fewer risks and will receive more benefits from our fellows if they share with us certain basic knowledge and beliefs. And in a country with democratic institutions there is the further important consideration that democracy is not likely to work, except on the smallest local scale, with a partly illiterate people.[86]

Hayek distances himself from the fascistic notion that mass education is altruistic by suggesting that the individual is at 'risk' from others, rather than at one with them, and the democratic participation he envisions is thus quite different from the old socialists' notion of 'ascetic, anti-materialistic, self-denying'[87] humanism. Rather than cultivating individuals' higher values for enlightened social participation through immersion in tradition, education for Hayek is an exercise in damage limitation. The idea that the primary function of cultural knowledge is to prevent children from being absorbed into an undifferentiated mass has been lent weight, intentionally or not, by educationalists such as E.D. Hirsch. According to Hirsch, children must learn the 'traditions of their society' in order to express their individuality.[88] Americans 'brought up under individualistic theories' are, he says, 'not less conventional than their predecessors, only less literate, less able to express their individuality'.[89] Hirsch describes progressive education as 'individualistic', no doubt because of its tendency to focus on the child at the centre of the learning experience, yet the traditional scholasticism favoured by Hirsch is profoundly individualistic, as noted by Dewey, and individualism is viewed by conservatives such as Rand is the antithesis of the irrational altruism of the "permissive society" that Hirsch presumably distains.

Conclusion

Sadie Plant notes the pessimism that has developed in the wake of postmodern theories of governance,[90] which identify a process of subordination that has obliged us to internalise mechanisms of control, erasing anything repellent to the controlling 'gaze'. Ironically, the terror of performativity, which seeks to eradicate fascistic altruism, has undermined the basis of the liberal tradition it purports to admire by inhibiting our ability to recognise and reject depersonalised relations as immoral (*see Chapter 4*). In consequence, something of a moral vacuum has been identified by Fenwick, who claims that teacher surveillance 'fragments and reduces human identity and experience, tearing people from material and social networks and targets for intervention'.[91] Foucault's analysis of power might lead us to conclude that the atomised and socially alienated self *is* the moral subject cultivated through neoliberal surveillance. Sentenced to death for neglecting a long-dormant law, Claudio remarks, 'Thus can the demigod, Authority, / Make us pay down for our offence by weight' (1.2.112–113). As we have seen, this "mortal-deity" hybrid is composed of Angelo's rationality and the Duke's spirituality, and has the power of life and death over the citizens of Vienna. In spite of the play's comical treatment of Barnardine and Pompey's refusal to worship this demi-god, the play's happy ending is dependent not upon individuals' intransigence, but upon their willingness to cast off disguise and duplicity and acknowledge the virtue of personalised relations – a phenomenon which is given greater explication by Shakespeare in *Antony and Cleopatra* (*see Chapter 4*). Thus, in *Measure for Measure*, slanders and subterfuge are forgiven, obligations to wronged lovers are publically acknowledged, and loyalty is rewarded. In the scales of justice evoked by the play's title, equilibrium is possible only when the power of high office does not outweigh the virtue of personalised relations. In light of Foucault's analysis, such equilibrium appears unlikely in the realm of contemporary education, where teachers are subjected to the neoliberal demi-god of Authority, whose power to eradicate "permissiveness" through the stimulation of our rational and spiritual self-governance obfuscates the extent to which social control outweighs human connectivity in the market society.

Notes

1 Ball, S. & Olmedo, A. (2013) 'Care of the Self, Resistance and Subjectivity under Neoliberal Governmentalities' *Critical Studies in Education*, *54* (1), pp. 85–96.
2 Ibid: 86.
3 Ball, S. (2003: 220) 'The Teacher's Soul and the Terrors of Performativity' *Journal of Education Policy*, *18* (2), pp. 215–228.
4 Ibid: 215.
5 Ball, S. (2012: 19) 'Performativity, Commodification and Commitment: An I-Spy Guide to the Neoliberal University' *British Journal of Educational Studies*, *60* (1), pp. 17–28.
6 Ibid.
7 Ibid.
8 Apple, M. (1995) *Education and Power*. Second Edition. London: Routledge. p. ix.
9 Ball, S. (2003: 217).
10 Tillyard, E.M.W. (1949) *Shakespeare's Problem Plays*. London: Chatto & Windus.
11 Stead, C.K. (1971) 'Introduction' In: Stead, C.K. (ed.) *Shakespeare: Measure for Measure. A Selection of Critical Essays*. London: The Macmillan Press Ltd. pp. 11–34.
12 Dollimore, J. (2003) 'Transgression and Surveillance in *Measure for Measure*' In: Dollimore, J. & Sinfield, A. (eds.) *Political Shakespeare: Essays in Cultural Materialism*. Second Edition. Manchester: Manchester University Press. pp. 72–87.
13 Foucault, M. (1994) *Power*. Faubion, J.S. (ed.) & Hurley, R. (trans.). London: Penguin Books Ltd.
14 Foucault (1994: 333).
15 Ibid: 213.
16 Gierke, O. in Bowle, J. (1961) *Western Political Thought*. London: Methuen & Co Ltd. p. 293.
17 Bowle (1961); Foucault (1994).
18 Hooker, R. in Dollimore, J. (2003: 81) 'Transgression and Surveillance in *Measure for Measure*' In: Dollimore, J. & Sinfield, A. (eds.) *Political Shakespeare: Essays in Cultural Materialism*. Second Edition. Manchester: Manchester University Press. pp. 72–87.
19 Ibid.
20 Holbrook, P. (2010) *Shakespeare's Individualism*. Cambridge: Cambridge University Press.
21 Robson, W.W. (1965) 'Shakespeare and His Modern Editors' In: Stead, C.K. (ed.) (1971) *Shakespeare: Measure for Measure*. London: The Macmillan Press Ltd. pp. 80–87.
22 Coleridge, S. (1827/1969: 274) '*Measure for Measure*: Comedy and Tragedy, a Hateful Play' In: Hawkes, T. (ed.) *Coleridge on Shakespeare*. Harmondsworth: Penguin Books Ltd. pp. 273–274.
23 West, M.R. & Peterson, P.E. (2003) 'The Politics and Practice of Accountability' In: West, M.R. & Peterson, P.E. (eds.) *No Child Left Behind? The Politics and Practice of School Accountability*. Washington, DC: Brookings Institution Press. pp. 1–20.
24 Ford, T.G., Van Sickle, M.E., Clark, L.V., Fazio-Brunson, M. & Schween, D.C. (2015) Teacher Self-Efficacy, Professional Commitment, and High-Stakes Teacher Evaluation Policy in Louisiana. *Educational Policy*. *1–47*. Available online at: http://epx.sagepub.com/content/early/2015/05/27/0895904815586855.full.pdf+html [Accessed 27th July 2015].
25 Maclure, S. (2000: 265) *The Inspectors' Calling: HMI and the Shaping of Educational Policy 1945–1992*. London: Hodder & Stoughton Ltd.

26 Fitz, J. & Lee, J. (1996: 17) 'Where Angels Fear . . .' In: Ousten, J., Earley, P. & Fidler, B. (eds.) *Ofsted Inspections: The Early Experience*. London: David Fulton Publishers Ltd. pp. 10–21.

27 Major, J. (1991) Conservative Party Conference Speech 1991. Available online at: http://www.johnmajor.co.uk/speechconf1991.html [Accessed 18th August 2010].

28 Jeffrey, B. & Woods, P. (1996: 334) 'Feeling Deprofessionalised: The Social Construction of Emotions during an OFSTED Inspection' *Cambridge Journal of Education, 26* (3), pp. 325–343.

29 Ibid.

30 Tuck, E. (2013: 341) 'Neoliberalism as Nihilism? A Commentary on Educational Accountability, Teacher Education, and School Reform' *The Journal for Critical Education Policy Studies, 11* (2), pp. 324–347.

31 Foucault, M. (1980) *Power/Knowledge: Selected Interviews and Other Writings, 1972–1977*. Gordon, C. (ed. & trans.). New York: Pantheon Press. p. 155.

32 Ibid.

33 Fenwick, T. (2003: 341) 'The "good" Teacher in a Neo-liberal Risk Society: A Foucaultian Analysis of Professional Growth Plans' *Journal of Curriculum Studies, 35* (3), pp. 335–354.

34 Ibid.

35 Ford et al (2015).

36 Ibid: 3.

37 Ibid.

38 Ibid.

39 Ibid: 26.

40 Ibid: 28.

41 Rand, A. (1964) *The Virtue of Selfishness*. New York: Signet.

42 Curtis, S.J. & Boultwood, M.E.A. (1966) *A Short History of Educational Ideas*. London: University Tutorial Press Ltd. p. 375.

43 Ibid: 466.

44 Dewey, J. (2011) *Democracy and Education*. www.simonandbrown.com

45 Curtis & Boultwood (1966: 471).

46 Dewey (2011).

47 Rhodes, C. (1998) *Structures of the Jazz Age*. London: Verso.

48 Ibid.

49 Ibid: 140.

50 Dewey (2011: 17).

51 Rand, A. (1964) *The Virtue of Selfishness*. New York, NY: Signet. p. 37.

52 Ibid: 38.

53 Dewey (2011: 17).

54 Roegele, O.B. (1994) 'Excerpt from *Die deutsche Universität im Dritten Reich*' In: Noakes, J. & Pridham, G. (eds.) *Nazism 1919–1945. Volume 2: State, Economy and Society 1933–1939*. Exeter: University of Exeter Press. pp. 442–443.

55 Heyen, F.J. (1994) 'Excerpt from *Nationalsozialismus im Alltag*' In: Noakes, J. & Pridham, G. (eds.) *Nazism 1919–1945. Volume 2: State, Economy and Society 1933–1939*. Exeter: University of Exeter Press. pp. 421–422.

56 Noakes, J. & Pridham, G. (1994) *Nazism 1919–1945. Volume 2: State, Economy and Society 1933–1939*. Exeter: University of Exeter Press.

57 Ibid: 441.

58 Ibid.

59 Paterson, L. (2015) *Social Radicalism and Liberal Education*. Exeter: Imprint Academic. p. 69.

60 Ibid: 54.

61 Arnold, M. (1869) *Culture and Anarchy*. Available online at: http://www.gutenberg. org/ebooks/4212?msg=welcome_stranger [Accessed 26th November 2015].
62 Marrou, H.I. (1964) *A History of Education in Antiquity*. Lamb, G. (trans.). New York, NY: A Mentor Book Published by The New American Library.
63 Ibid: 131.
64 Dale, R. (1979) 'From Endorsement to Disintegration: Progressive Education from the Golden Age to the Green Paper' *British Journal of Educational Studies*, *27*(3), pp. 191–209.
65 Westbrook, R.B. (1993) 'John Dewey (1859–1952)' *Prospects: The Quarterly Review of Comparative Education, XXIII* (1\2), pp. 277–291.
66 Illich, I. (2015) *Deschooling Society*. London: Marion Boyars Publishers Ltd.
67 Dale (1979: 196).
68 Young, M.F.D. (ed.) *Knowledge and Control: New Directions for the Sociology of Education*. London: Collier-Macmillan.
69 Boronski, T. & Hassan, N. (2015) *Sociology of Education*. London: SAGE Publications Ltd. p. 53.
70 Paterson (2015: 167).
71 Rose, J. (2002) *The Intellectual Life of the British Working Classes*. New Haven, CT: Yale University Press. p. 281.
72 Ibid.
73 What's new? *The Guardian*. Available online at: http://www.theguardian.com/ education/2001/oct/16/schools.uk [Accessed 20th May 2015].
74 Friedman, M. (2002) *Capitalism and Freedom: 40th Anniversary Edition*. Chicago: The University of Chicago Press.
75 Dewey (2011).
76 Apple (1995).
77 Fairfield, P. (2009) *Education after Dewey*. London: Continuum International Publishing Group. p. 239.
78 Thatcher, M. (1987) 'Interview for Woman's Own'. Available online at: http:// www.margaretthatcher.org/speeches/displaydocument.asp?docid=106689 [Accessed 26th November 2015].
79 Fairfield (2009: 239).
80 Dewey (2011: 17).
81 Ibid: 183.
82 Ibid.
83 Hayek, F.A. (2007) *The Road to Serfdom. Text and Documents: The Definitive Edition*. Chicago: The University of Chicago Press. p. 499.
84 Ibid: 115.
85 Ibid.
86 Hayek, F.A. (2011) *The Constitution of Liberty: The Definitive Edition*. Hamowy, R. (ed.). Chicago: The University of Chicago Press.
87 Krammick, I. & Sherman, B. (1993: 158) *Harold Laski*. London: Hamish Hamilton, cited in: Paterson (2015: 49).
88 Hirsch, E.D. (1987) *Cultural Literacy: What Every American Needs to Know*. Boston: Houghton Mifflin Company. p. 126.
89 Ibid.
90 Plant, S. (1997) *The Most Radical Gesture*. London: Routledge.
91 Fenwick (2003: 341).

3   School leadership
Macbeth

Introduction

In *The Road to Serfdom*, Hayek claimed that 'The Nazi leader who described the National Socialist revolution as counter-Renaissance spoke more truly than he probably knew'.[1] Totalitarianism, according to Hayek, is antithetical to individualism, which he defines as 'respect for the individual man *qua* man, that is, the recognition of his own views and tastes as supreme in his own sphere, however narrowly that may be circumscribed, and the belief that it is desirable that men should develop their own individual gifts and bents'.[2] Hayek identified the Renaissance as the source of this 'Tolerance' of freedom, which, he claims, 'only in recent times has again been in decline, to disappear completely with the rise of the totalitarian state'.[3] In Chapter 1, the status of Hamlet as the emblematic 'first modern man'[4] was acknowledged, and his attempt to resist the suffocation of the Danish court was considered in light of the neoliberal conceptualisation of the "heroic" entrepreneur, whose potency is likewise jeopardised by the control of risk. When thinking about the entrepreneur as an 'individual man *qua* man', Antony Jay also looked back, like Hayek, to the Renaissance.[5] Jay's ground-breaking book, *Management and Machiavelli*, published in 1967, drew inspiration from Niccolò Machiavelli's Renaissance masterpiece, *The Prince*, and helped popularise Machiavelli's leadership theory contemporaneously with the ascension of neoliberalism. Since the 1980s, the promotion of human capital theory in education policy has introduced this corporate ideology into the discourse of education.[6] Head teachers have been duly recast as school *leaders*,[7] and traditional forms of school administration that oblige schoolteachers to maintain legal norms with integrity under a public service ethos have been replaced by an increase in 'consumer control'[8] of education under an 'accountability ethos'.[9] Accordingly, the idea that educators are public servants committed to the public good has been replaced by the idea that the professions (e.g. teachers, doctors, lawyers) are 'self-interested groups who indulge in rent-seeking behaviour'.[10] This loss of faith in the moral authority of institutions has gone hand-in-glove with the elevation of our collective admiration of executive power, and thus while today we distrust "big government", we are ready to salute individuals whose pursuit of self-interest has been crowned by achievement.

Shakespeare, like most of his contemporaries, was familiar with Machiavelli's *The Prince*,[11] and indeed the Machiavellian pursuit of political self-interest is a significant feature of Shakespeare's history plays.[12] *Macbeth* is described by Reginald A. Foakes as 'Shakespeare's last and most original play on the theme of the ambitious prince finally overthrown',[13] and it seethes with Machiavellian duplicity and instrumentality. In a virtuoso display of political cunning, the Macbeths devise a plan to win the crown of Scotland by playing the congenial hosts to King Duncan; murdering him in his bed and throwing suspicion on his sons. This abandonment of moral law under the cloak of virtue delivers material success in line with Machiavelli's hypothesis, but the tragic conclusion of *Macbeth* draws our attention to the limitations of this creed. Macbeth, unlike Hamlet, could never be described as a 'sweet prince', and it is perhaps surprising that educators today have been encouraged to adopt the leadership strategy of a Shakespearean villain. The aim of this chapter is to consider, through a reading of *Macbeth*, our elevation of the school *leader* and what it means to be 'an individual man *qua* man'.

The Prince

The Prince's central message (considered scandalous in the sixteenth century) is that successful leaders adapt their instincts to new events.[14] In other words, success is not dependent upon the possession of virtues such as wisdom and honour, but on *flexibility*. According to Machiavelli, the successful leader has 'a mind ready to turn itself accordingly as the winds and variations of fortune force it' and sticks to the good if he can, but 'if compelled' knows how to be bad and is willing 'to set about it'.[15] Machiavelli implies that the executive who exercises control and imposes order is resolutely male, while Fortune is female and open to seduction by the determined leader. For English readers, the degree of sexual violence in Machiavelli's writing varies according to its translation. For example, John Roe's translation employs language associated with rape: he states, 'Fortune is a woman, and the man who wants to hold her down must beat and bully her'.[16] The translation by Tim Parks is less brutal: he states, 'fortune is female and if you want to stay on top of her you have to slap and thrust'.[17] No matter how cautiously it is translated, however, Machiavelli's theory implies that the successful leader is virile.

Famously, Machiavelli advised the prince 'to play the fox to see the snares and the lion to scare off the wolves'.[18] The successful leader is adaptable: he is not simply a 'fox' or a 'lion' but knows how to mimic both. Machiavelli devotes an entire chapter of *The Prince* to an analysis of states won through crime, and the thrust of his argument is that leaders must be willing to demonstrate 'violence and cruelty'[19] at all times, and should only indulge their desire to model virtues such as generosity when it is prudent to do so. According to Harvey C. Mansfield, Machiavelli was prepared to advocate this disregard for the spiritual consequences that might follow the abandonment of moral law because he did not believe that God or nature may be 'relied on to help execute men's laws, there being no natural law or natural right behind those laws'.[20] If there is no God to condemn sinners to eternal damnation, then it is sufficient for us to display the *appearance* of what Machiavelli describes as 'greatness, spirit, seriousness and strength'[21] in order to gain sway over others. For Machiavelli, the actual possession of these virtues is immaterial. Famously, *The Prince* was considered so seditious that it was banned by the Pope in 1559, but the question that it raises continued to tantalise Renaissance Europe: if flexibility ensures power, should we favour the appearance of virtue over the rigid adherence to moral law?

Macbeth

Macbeth might be described as a nightmare of moral flexibility. Lady Macbeth is delighted when witches foretell that her husband, Macbeth, will become King of Scotland. Eager to turn the wheel of fortune herself, rather than let a Machiavellian prince take the initiative, Lady Macbeth decides that she will importune her husband to assassinate King Duncan and seize the crown. A true apostle of Machiavelli, Lady Macbeth believes that the ability to conceal the propensity for 'violence and cruelty'[22] behind a façade of gentility is essential to effective leadership, and that this propensity is fundamentally male. Lady Macbeth therefore seeks to liberate her hidden psychology from her outwardly perceptible gender in order to access what she believes to be the masculine ability to 'Look like th' innocent flower, / But be the serpent under't' (1.5.63–64), in a female variation of Machiavelli's fox and lion metaphor. Without this psychic liberation, Lady Macbeth will remain an inert 'flower'; the passive recipient of what she calls 'visitings of nature' (1.5.43), like the rose visited by the bee, and she duly cries out to the spirits, 'unsex me here' (1.5.49).

The depiction of witchcraft is perhaps the most celebrated feature of *Macbeth*, and during Shakespeare's time it was common for men to worry about women's occult tendencies; indeed, in 1597 the future King James I (for whom *Macbeth* was first performed) published his own panic-stricken treatise on witchcraft, the *Demonologie*.[23] It was widely believed that by casting spells and administering potions, women could cause weakness, disease and death, and that the source of women's occult power resided in the birthing chamber.[24] As noted by Duby et al., masculine power ended on the threshold of the birthing chamber where children were conceived and born and where the sick were brought to die: 'In this most private sanctum, woman ruled over the dark realm of sexual pleasure, reproduction, and death'.[25] It is this mystique of the birthing chamber, replete with images of menstruation, gestation, lactation and death, that Lady Macbeth invokes in her infamous call to the 'spirits' to divest her of femininity. By calling upon supernatural forces to un-gender her, Lady Macbeth resembles in psychic form the sexually ambiguous witches who prophesy that Macbeth shall wear the crown of Scotland. These 'weird sisters' (1.3.33) have female bodies yet bearded faces, and from this we might surmise that the witches and Lady Macbeth hold masculine power, but that their attainment of agency is a diabolical transgression of nature that takes women away from their "natural" form.

Initially, Macbeth is reluctant to engage in the subterfuge proposed by his "de-sexed" wife for two reasons: first, he has been 'honoured . . . of late' by Duncan (1.7.32), and thus feels a debt of gratitude. Second, Macbeth wishes to maintain the 'Golden opinions from all sorts of people' (1.7.33) that he has lately won. We have no reason to doubt Macbeth's "masculine" appetite for violence: prior to his arrival onstage, we are told that Macbeth has 'unseam'd' a man 'from the nave to th' chops' (1.2.22). Clearly, Macbeth is not squeamish, and we may therefore surmise that it is Macbeth's desire to personify, rather than mimic, fidelity that makes him balk at regicide. As stated previously, Machiavelli implies that instrumental behaviour is manly, and Lady Macbeth takes this gendering one step further by implying that the desire to combine the appearance of virtue with actual goodness is effeminate. Lady Macbeth reminds her husband of his previ-ous willingness to kill King Duncan, saying 'When you durst do it, then you were a man' (1.7.49), and conflates his current prevarication with sexual dysfunction. By goading her husband to express his masculinity through murder, Lady Mac-beth demonstrates her conviction that effective leaders are male and are willing and able to seize Fortune, who is female. For Lady Macbeth, only impotent men want to align their inner and outer goodness, and her contempt for this 'green and pale' (1.7. 37) virginal sentiment succeeds in inspiring Macbeth to commit regicide.

L.C. Knights argues that *Macbeth* is a play that dwells upon the notion that 'the man who breaks the bonds that tie him to other men' is at the same time 'violating his own nature and thwarting his own deepest needs'.[26] This idea of violation rests, of course, upon the assumption that there is a 'nature' to be violated; a theory which Machiavelli rejects. As stated previously, for Machiavelli a leader who wins a state through crime cannot be said to be violating his own nature, as there is no essential self, only a series of choices that have better and worse outcomes for the individual. Since there is no divine or natural law to be breeched, no behaviour may be deemed essentially wrong, only wrongly used. If Machiavelli is correct, then Macbeth does not violate divine law by killing a man to whom he felt a debt of gratitude, and therefore has no reason to fear esoteric sanction for behaviour that is *pragmatically* sound. However, Macbeth's inability to hold together his inner and outer selves constitutes a "natural" impediment to this moral flexibility, and in the banqueting scene that marks the beginning of Macbeth's loss of power,[27] Shakespeare provides a dramatic study of the fraught yet inescapable relationship between sincerity and subterfuge. This choice of set-ting is highly significant, as medieval banquets were subject to a strict decorum that was intended to ensure that the family was shown off to advantage while 'pri-vate secrets remained hidden beneath a splendid façade'.[28] Macbeth is thwarted in this venture by his conscience, which projects grotesque visions into the private realm of his mind to disrupt his outward projection of propriety. Upon seeing the ghost of one of his murder victims at the banquet, Macbeth babbles incoherently before his guests, and Lady Macbeth chides her husband for being 'unmann'd in folly' (3.4.75). This time, Lady Macbeth's suggestion that troubled minds are effeminate does not inspire her husband to embrace masculine Machiavellian flexibility. Instead, Macbeth commits the grand *faux-pas* of quitting the banquet ahead of his guests in a symbolic rendering of his 'golden' public image and his murderous private self.

By consulting the witches and responding to his wife's goading, Macbeth allows the mystique of the birthing chamber to enter his psyche with disastrous results: steeped in blood spilled through murder rather than birth, Macbeth suffers a hideous vision of a bloody child and is subsequently killed by a man who was ripped from his mother's womb. Macbeth's ultimate failure as a leader speaks not, however, of the hazards of women's occult power, but of the Macbeths' breach of divine and natural law.

Machiavellianism and neoliberalism

Reflecting on the popularity of Machiavelli's theory in the business sector, Peter J. Galie and Christopher Bopst argue that an application of his ideas would suggest that one 'cannot be a decent human being following Judeo-Christian ethics, including the laws derived therefrom, and simultaneously build a successful corporate enterprise',[29] as these are 'un-combinable and incommensurable values, virtues and moralities'.[30] The incompatibility of Judeo-Christian ethics and Machiavellian corporate activity is, however, immaterial to exponents of neoliberalism. Indeed, if we subscribe to Rand's secular conception of man as a 'volitional consciousness',[31] we might feel irritated by Shakespeare's depiction of supernatural beings in both *Macbeth* and *Hamlet*. In these plays, spectral visions and magical divinations challenge the primacy of rationality as our source of knowledge, and the idea that corporate enterprises should be directed by mystical beliefs might, perhaps, be legitimately dismissed by followers of Rand as anti-rational. Conversely, if we subscribe to Hayek's anti-rationalistic theory of the Great Society, we might be inclined to reject the divine and natural law depicted in *Macbeth* as manifestations of the medieval belief that altruism and solidarity are the keystones of social order. According to Hayek, socialism's archaic discourse of interdependence threatens the future of Western civilisation by failing to acknowledge that technological progress has been made possible through creative individuals' cooperation with *abstract* rules of conduct, rather than compliance with *concrete* common aims.[32] Indeed, Andrew Gamble notes that for Hayek, socialism is a reactionary, anti-modernist doctrine that reasserts the kind of pre-modern 'tribal ethics'[33] that are violated by the Macbeths. Whether rationalists or not, followers of neoliberalism are unlikely to find much to admire in the quasi-religious condemnation of instrumentality in *Macbeth*.

Although neoliberalism, like Machiavellianism, challenges the validity of the pre-modern concept of divine and natural law, Hayek was outspoken about the danger of freedom unconstrained by ethics.[34] According to Hayek:

> It is indeed a truth, which all great apostles of freedom outside the rationalistic school have never tired of emphasizing, that freedom has never worked without deeply engrained moral beliefs and that coercion can be reduced

to a minimum only where individuals can be expected as a rule to conform voluntarily to certain principles.[35]

As discussed in Chapter 1, Hayek's theory of the "natural selection" of behaviours that support and maintain the Great Society is predicated upon the assumption that human reason is insufficient to grasp the complexity of reality, making it prudent for us to 'submit to the common rules of action which have been evolved through the social process'.[36] In the West, these rules, whether sacred or secular in origin, constitute the liberal tradition that must be upheld to prevent anarchy, and conforming to these principles requires little reflection on our part, as for Hayek, 'the system of values into which we are born supplies the ends which our reason must serve'.[37] Unlike divine and natural law, these values are not held to be important because they are universal "truths", but because they have played a vital role in the "survival of the fittest" elements of our society. As noted by Gamble, Hayek saw himself as pragmatic, rather than unprincipled: believing that it is not possible to make society good by making it behave morally, Hayek argued that 'we must endeavour to make society good in the sense that we shall like to live in it'.[38] For Hayek this good society is, of course, the market society.

The market society

For exponents of market individualism, society is comprised of individuals 'uncontrolled by any single will',[39] who are engaged in 'myriads of independent transactions'.[40] By expressing our individual preferences through organisational units, and through the interaction of these units with each other, the disordered expression of our individual values becomes a 'social choice'.[41] Under the market mechanism, our preferences are tallied to determine the 'market leader', and outcomes are deemed to 'accord with the preferences of the sum total of economic agents'.[42] It is commonly held that the corporate world is 'nature red in tooth and claw',[43] and by imagining that values are simply *preferences* and encouraging individuals to express their preferences through such things as consumer satisfaction surveys, the market mechanism appears to guarantee that the preferences of 'wolves' do not assume greater significance than the preferences of 'doves'.[44]

It is widely acknowledged that Machiavelli founded the modern doctrine of executive power,[45] yet in *The Prince* he argues that a successful leader capitalises upon disorder to impose his will on the multitude. From this we might surmise that there is an irrevocable tension between the market mechanism's preclusion of one person's ability to exert his or her will over another, and Machiavelli's conception of the executive as a totalitarian leader. This apparent contradiction is, however, ostensibly resolved through the application of the market mechanism in the public sector; a phenomenon that has come to be known as new public management (NPM). In the realm of education, NPM has attempted to transform the moral landscape of pedagogy by abandoning traditional forms of school administration, which oblige school leaders to maintain legal norms with integrity under a 'public service' ethos, and replacing them with a system of 'consumer control' of education under an 'accountability ethos'.[46] This consumer control, which ostensibly precludes the kind of individuated power admired by Machiavelli, is made possible through two mechanisms: first, the establishment of "consumer groups", such as school governing councils, and second, the public scrutiny of schools' performance through league tables. Under the accountability ethos, the school leader must deal impartially with the various consumer groups that have been established under NPM in order for individuals to expresses their preferences (e.g. school councils; parents' groups), and to be effective, she must employ Machiavellian guile to navigate a successful route for her school through the micro-political environment of centrally imposed standards and consumer demands.[47] The complexity of this arrangement has, in theory, fostered a 'collective or distributed approach to leadership'[48] in which negotiation is of paramount importance. Thus tamed by the market mechanism, Machiavellianism promises to yield an executive whose moral flexibility ensures power for the *organisation*, rather than herself.

The idea that market relations are inherently anti-totalitarian is, however, open to question. In *Just Money*, Ann Pettifor critiques the "mythology" of the ethically neutral free market, claiming that:

> By detaching social relationships from regulation, and allowing them to be enforced by the 'invisible hand' of the abstract 'market' – regulators, economists and bankers abdicated their responsibility for upholding and defending society's moral and ethical standards.[49]

In line with Hayek's philosophy, concrete social aims have been abandoned in favour of the abstract aims of the market, but this revolution has not led to the Adam Smith-style harmony of interests envisaged by Hayek. Instead, we have witnessed the emergence of what Dale Rubin describes as 'corporate personhood'.[50] According to Rubin, US courts have enabled corporations to gain 'unprecedented power'[51] over the body politic by granting them constitutional rights intended for individuals. As Machiavellian "princes", these corporations are unfettered by concern for divine and natural law, and deregulation has thus released them from legal control, which was their only restraint. As a result, the power wielded by these latter-day princes is immense. For example, the investor-state dispute resolution (ISDS) gives foreign investors the ability to sue a government for legislation that harms their investment – a phenomenon that resulted in the notorious legal challenge to the Australian government's decision to introduce plain cigarette packaging in 2012.[52] In this instance, a tobacco "prince" figuratively declared war on a presumptuous foreign state – a strategy highly recommended by Machiavelli in his guide to autocratic power. In light of such behaviour, we might question the suitability of the market mechanism as a means to limit coercion.

The school leader

In *The Prince*, Machiavelli acknowledged that his contemporaries' deep-seated belief in divine and natural law might make his theory seem unworkable – a sentiment echoed by Eustace Tillyard, who claimed that in Shakespeare's time,

Machiavelli's 'day had not yet come'.[53] Today, however, we might say that Machiavelli's time *has* come, as his theory chimes with and indeed informs the neoliberal hegemony. We might note in particular the resonance between Machiavelli's analysis of the historic actions of successful leaders and Hayek's interest in social evolution. Rejecting divine and natural law as the foundation of human interaction, Machiavelli offered an analysis of cause and effect to produce a quasi-scientific account of the executive whose success is dependent upon his willingness to *adapt* to new events. In keeping with Hayek's anti-rationalistic philosophy, literature on school leadership tends to hail Machiavelli's advice as prudent simply because it is pragmatic. For example, in *Learning How to Lead in Higher Education*, Paul Ramsden states:

> Machiavelli was nothing if not pragmatic. Instead of trying to establish what was right and wrong about power and leadership, as so many others have done before and since, he looked at what worked. He examined practical problems facing leaders and offered advice based on the analysis of empirical data. He believed that leaders could learn how to lead if they studied the experiences of others before them.[54]

The "analysis of empirical data" offered by Machiavelli includes the instruction to destroy an invaded city; attack and disperse its population and eradicate 'its freedoms and traditions'[55] so that the population will not rise up to 'fight for those principles'.[56] We might question the virtue of basing school leadership theory on the tactics of warriors bent on destroying a city and suppressing its principles, although this might be a fitting metaphor for the neoliberals' attack on the permissive society and progressive education, discussed in the preceding chapters.

In homage to Machiavelli, Fenwick W. English claims that 'The secondary school principal is an educational executive and, as such, is governed by the ideas of who and what an executive is and does'.[57] Perhaps not surprisingly, therefore, in his study of contemporary school leadership James Ryan has uncovered examples of "successful" leadership that combine Machiavellian flexibility with belligerence. For example:

> Brenda is an experienced principal with many resources at her disposal. She knows that she "makes people nervous" and does not hesitate to use aggressive tactics when she can get away with it.[58]

As we have seen, aggression is advocated by Machiavelli as a leadership tactic, yet aggression is perhaps a surprising attribute to laud in educational settings. In spite of Shakespeare's powerful refutation of the notion that it is sufficient for a leader to *appear* virtuous, Machiavelli's advice about deception also appears to find favour with school leaders today. Consider, for example, Whitaker's counsel in *What Great Principals do Differently*, which reads like a paraphrase of *The Prince*:

> Every year, it was my practice to remind my faculty: "You don't have to like the students; you just have to act as if you like them." The reason is simple:

If you don't act as if you like them, your students won't think you care for them, even if you do. And if you act as if you like them, then your true feelings towards them are irrelevant.[59]

It is difficult to imagine a scenario in which our 'true feelings' towards other people are ever 'irrelevant', and the study of *Macbeth* indicates that enmity and subterfuge are more than superficially distasteful. For Knights, the cry of 'show like those you are' (5.6.1) is the central motif of *Macbeth*, and this cry is not a request but an imperative, as to connect with others we must show ourselves to them, rather than hide behind the kind of façade recommended by Whitaker. Such connectivity is, of course, deemed irrelevant in *The Prince*. Mansfield notes that in Machiavelli's writing, conspiracy isolates the leader as '*uno solo*',[60] the 'one alone' who is individuated by his pursuit of glory, and he contrasts Machiavelli's idea that conspiracy underlies all politics with the classical view, put forward by Aristotle, that friendship underlies all justice and all politics. Another Renaissance figure, Michel de Montaigne, echoes Aristotle, saying, 'There is nothing Nature seems to have led us to more than to society'.[61] Macbeth blatantly disregards this injunction of nature: having butchered his King, conspired against the King's sons and murdered his own comrades, he learns of the death of Lady Macbeth, his co-conspirator and 'partner in greatness' (1.5.9). Isolated by conspiracy and now truly alone, Macbeth does not lament the loss of his lover and his closest ally, but instead proclaims his weariness with 'th'estate o'th' world' (5.6.50). As though anticipating the absurdist stance that everything is meaningless in a meaningless universe, Macbeth derides human existence as 'a tale / Told by an idiot, full of sound and fury / Signifying nothing' (5.5.24–28). Ultimately, Machiavellian flexibility ossifies Macbeth, who is unable to do anything more than press onwards with cruelty under the belief that all behaviours are equally devoid of meaning.

The 'individual man *qua* man'

This, then, is the 'individual man *qua* man' admired by Hayek: unhindered by the "folklore" of divine and natural law, he is never more than pragmatically connected to others, from whose preferences he is protected by the market. Liberated from the illusion of society, he is free to focus his gaze inwards, to recognise 'his own views and tastes as supreme in his own sphere, however narrowly that may be circumscribed'[62] and to develop his 'own individual gifts and bents'.[63] Willing to bear risk in the market society and to shoulder the burden of his own endeavours for good or ill, this self-cultivated 'man *qua* man' seeks nothing from his fellow man beyond the right to express his preferences, and is willing to employ Machiavellian guile in order to further his cause. Hayek acknowledged that ethics have no part to play in the market mechanism beyond the inhibition of totalitarianism.[64] Consequently, in the market society there is no concept of "just rewards", and a duplicitous braggart may prosper while a humble and honest man does not, making Machiavellianism both ethically sound and judicious.

Hayek identifies the Renaissance as the starting point for this conceptualisation of the "liberated" man, and clearly there is a resonance between Hayek's notion of self-actualisation and the concept of the Renaissance scholar. There is, perhaps, more than a hint of constraint in the Emperor Marcus Aurelius Antoninus' second-century testimony that, 'We are made for cooperation, like feet, like hands, like eyelids, like the rows of the upper and lower teeth'[65] and that to act against one another is therefore 'contrary to nature'.[66] Certainly, the medieval conception of society as a single organism, guided to salvation through knowledge of God's law, was challenged during the Renaissance by the idea of the *self* as a discrete unit developed through study,[67] and as we have seen, this desire for self-actualisation is a prominent theme in both *Hamlet* and *Macbeth*. However, this ideological shift did not displace Christ as the foundation of reason,[68] and in spite of the publication of *The Prince* in the 16th century, Adorno and Horkheimer argue that it was not until the scientific revolution of the seventeenth century that a 'factual mentality'[69] began to emerge. Adorno and Horkheimer acknowledge Shakespeare's contemporary, Francis Bacon, as the father of experimental philosophy, and claim that Bacon's belief that nature is something that might be used by men to dominate others led to a disenchantment of the world that culminated in the Enlightenment's reduction of all 'mythic figures'[70] to the human subject. Bacon's belief that "knowledge is power" is still upheld today, but the nature of this knowledge is highly specific. According to Adorno and Horkheimer, Enlightenment thinking has encouraged us to believe that 'the supernatural, spirits and demons, are mirror images of men who allow themselves to be frightened by natural phenomena'.[71] Under this world view, supernatural visitations cannot be considered to be a conduit to knowledge, as depicted in *Hamlet* and *Macbeth*, as the very concept of the supernatural is a manifestation of our ignorance of the true nature of phenomena. Bacon hypothesised that by dispelling our ignorance we may obtain power over nature, and modern Machiavellians are likely to adopt a scientific strategy to discern what Friedman describes as the 'objective'[72] laws of positive economics and thus wield power in the market. These economic rules are considered to be natural, in that they are 'independent of any ethical opinion or normative judgement',[73] but have no mystical basis. Perhaps most importantly, the objective laws of positive economics are ostensibly discoverable by any inquiring mind, and the alleged impartiality of the scientific method helps explain the disinclination on the part of figures such as Hayek and Friedman to view the market mechanism as biased, in spite of the obvious discrepancy of information-as-power held by corporate "princes" and their "subjects".

School leadership for equity

Policy on school leadership has developed internationally in response to concern over social and economic inequalities, and has been implemented by governments as a means to identify and exclude factors that might otherwise inhibit national education performance.[74] At first glance, the idea of 'school leadership for equity'[75] appears to be at odds with neoliberalism's emphasis on individual rather than collective responsibility for personal well-being,[76] and indeed policy on school leadership for equity has been welcomed by many educationalists as a reprieve from neoliberalism's insistence on rampant individualism.[77] A closer look at policy on school leadership for equity reveals, however, that social justice has been firmly established in the neoliberal discourse as 'a private matter that requires behavioural management',[78] rather than a collective concern that warrants political action. Consequently, social justice is theorised in education policy documents as the 'removal of barriers to engagement and achievement'[79] that might otherwise inhibit disadvantaged pupils' ability to 'participate, engage and succeed in various aspects of mainstream life',[80] rather than 'the radical revision of mainstream life'.[81] This perspective is consistent with the belief that social problems are amenable to the kind of scientific scrutiny advocated by Bacon, and that it is possible to discover the "laws of educational attainment" and thus gain mastery over them. Presumably, school leaders who possess knowledge of how and why children fail academically may wield its attendant power to modify the behaviour of their pupils and thereby enhance the position of their schools in performance league tables. This approach to social justice equates "success" with the personal efficacy of individual school leaders, measured through their organisation's relative performance, making it entirely consistent with Machiavellian individualism.

It seems that the pre-modern concept of divine and natural law has, like witchcraft, been dismissed under neoliberalism as a relic from the Middle Ages – a dismal period from which we have been mercifully delivered through the process of social evolution, as identified by Hayek. In *Management and Machiavelli*, Jay says, 'It is strange that Shakespeare, who had such a profound insight into so many corners of the human heart, should never have understood the nature of the leader.'[82] In response to Jay's assessment of Shakespeare's understanding of leadership, we might point out that Shakespeare acknowledges the tendency to reject any admonition of Machiavellianism. Lady Macduff, as a counterpoint to Lady Macbeth, offers a bleak appraisal of the Machiavellian landscape that accommodates Jay's cynicism, saying, 'I am in this earthly world – where to do harm / Is often laudable, to do good sometime / Accounted dangerous folly' (4.2. 75–77). As we have seen, school leaders today are praised for being duplicitous and aggressive in their pursuit of an anti-social concept of social justice, and in light of *Macbeth*, we might describe the idea of leadership for *equity* in this aggregate of competing individuals to be not only an impossible dream but a contradiction in terms. In conclusion, then, unless we are willing to agree with Jay that, with regard to leadership, Shakespeare simply "got it wrong", we should be concerned by the call for school principals to reinvent themselves as Machiavellian executives in the pursuit of social justice.

Notes

1 Hayek, F.A. (2007) *The Road to Serfdom. Text and Documents: The Definitive Edition*. Chicago: The University of Chicago Press. p. 68.

2 Ibid.
3 Ibid.
4 Rossiter, A.P. (1961) *Angel with Horns and Other Shakespeare Lectures*. New York: Theatre Arts Books. p. 187.
5 Jay, A. (1967) *Management and Machiavelli*. London: Hodder & Stoughton Ltd.
6 Alexiadou, N. (2011) 'Social Inclusion and Leadership in Education: An Evolution of Roles and Values in the English Education System over the Last 60 Years' *Education Inquiry*, 2 (4), pp. 581–600.
7 Ibid.
8 Mulford, B. (2003) 'School Leaders: Changing Roles and Impact on Teacher and School Effectiveness' Paper commissioned by the Education and Training Policy Division, OECD, for the Activity 'Attracting, Developing and Retaining Effective Teachers'. pp. 7–8. Available online at: http://www.learningdomain.com/Leadership.Sch.Effievct.pdf [Accessed 20th June 2014]
9 Ibid.
10 Olssen, M. & Peters, M.A. (2005: 325) 'Neoliberalism, Higher Education and the Knowledge Economy: From the Free Market to Knowledge Capitalism' *Journal of Education Policy*, 20 (3), pp. 313–345.
11 Lewis, W. (1927) *The Lion and the Fox: The Role of the Hero in the Plays of Shakespeare*. London: Grant Richards Ltd.
12 Tillyard, E.M.W. (1964) *Shakespeare's History Plays*. London: Chatto & Windus.
13 Foakes, R.A. (2005: 7) 'Images of Death: Ambition in *Macbeth*' In: Brown, J.R. (ed.) *Focus on Macbeth*. Abingdon: Routledge. pp. 7–29.
14 Parks, T. (2009) 'Introduction' In: Machiavelli, N. (ed.) *The Prince*. Parks, T. (trans.). London: Penguin Books Ltd.
15 Machiavelli, N. (2016) *The Prince*. Marriott, W.K. (trans.). Available online at: http://www.gutenberg.org/files/1232/1232-h/1232-h.htm [Accessed 28th April 2016].
16 Roe, J. (2002) *Shakespeare and Machiavelli*. Cambridge: D.S. Brewer. p. 1.
17 Machiavelli, N. (2009) *The Prince*. Parks, T. (trans. & intro.) London: Penguin Books Ltd. p. 101.
18 Machiavelli (2009: 69).
19 Ibid: 36.
20 Mansfield, H.C. (1998) *Machiavelli's Virtue*. Chicago: The University of Chicago Press. p. 301.
21 Machiavelli (2009: 72).
22 Ibid: 36.
23 Greenblatt, S. (2004) *Will in the World: How Shakespeare Became Shakespeare*. London: Jonathan Cape. p. 343.
24 Duby, G., Barthélemy, D. & de La Roncière, C. (1988) 'Portraits' In: Duby, G. (ed.) *A History of Private Life, Volume II: Revelations of the Medieval World*. Harvard: The Belknap Press. pp. 33–309.
25 Duby et al (1988: 80).
26 Knights, L.C. (1966) *Some Shakespearian Themes and an Approach to 'Hamlet'*. Stanford: Stanford University Press. p. 125.
27 Hawkins, M. (2005) 'History, Politics and *Macbeth*' In: Brown, J.R. (ed.) *Focus on Macbeth*. Abingdon: Routledge. pp. 155–188.
28 Duby et al (1988: 298).
29 Galie, P.J. & Bopst, C. (2006: 237) 'Machiavelli & Modern Business: Realist Thought in Contemporary Corporate Leadership Manuals' *Journal of Business Ethics*, 65, pp. 235–250.
30 Ibid.
31 Rand, A. (2007) *Atlas Shrugged*. London: Penguin Books Ltd. p. 1012.
32 Gamble, A. (1996) *Hayek: The Iron Cage of Liberty*. Cambridge: Polity Press.
33 Ibid: 45.

34   Hayek, F.A. (2011) *The Constitution of Liberty: The Definite Edition*. Hamowy, R. (ed.). Chicago: The University of Chicago Press.
35   Ibid: 123.
36   Ibid: 128.
37   Ibid: 124.
38   Hayek in Gamble (1996: 46).
39   Marquand, D. (2014) *Mammon's Kingdom: An Essay on Britain, Now*. London: Allen Lane. p. 49.
40   Ibid.
41   Enteman, W.F. (1993) *Managerialism: The Emergence of a New Ideology*. Madison, WI: The University of Wisconsin Press. p. 157.
42   Marquand (2014: 77).
43   Galie & Bopst (2006: 242).
44   Ibid.
45   Mansfield (1998: 314).
46   Mulford (2003: 7–8).
47   Ryan, J. (2012) *Struggling for Inclusion: Educational Leadership in a Neoliberal World*. Charlotte, NC: Information Age Publishing, Inc. p. 118.
48   Earley, P. (2013) *Exploring the School Leadership Landscape: Changing Demands, Changing Realities*. London: Bloomsbury Academic. p. 70.
49   Pettifor, A. (2014) *Just Money: How Society Can Break the Despotic Power of Finance*. Commonwealth-publishing.com. p. 26.
50   Rubin, D. (2009) 'Corporate Personhood: How the Courts Have Employed Bogus Jurisprudence to Grant Corporations Constitutional Rights Intended for Individuals' *Quinnipiac Law Review, 28* (523), pp. 523–584.
51   Ibid: 524.
52   Inman, P. (2016) 'A Deal for Freer Trade or Corporate Greed? Here's the Truth about TTIP' *The Observer* 1st March 2016, p. 36.
53   Tillyard (1964: 23).
54   Ramsden, P. (2000) *Learning to Lead in Higher Education*. London: Routledge. p. xii.
55   Machiavelli (2009: 19).
56   Ibid: 20.
57   English, F.W. (1992: 10) 'The Principal and the Prince: Machiavelli and School Leadership' *NASSP Bulletin, 76* (540), pp. 10–15.
58   Ryan (2012: 133).
59   Whitaker, T. (2012) *What Great Principals Do Differently: 18 Things That Matter Most*. Second Edition. Larchmont, NY: Eye on Education. p. 29.
60   Mansfield (1998: 312).
61   Montaigne, M. (2012) *Montaigne Selected Essays*. Atkinson, J.B & Sices, D. (trans.) & Atkinson, J.B. (Intro. & Notes). Indianapolis, IN: Hackett Publishing Company, Inc. p. 74.
62   Hayek (2007: 68).
63   Ibid.
64   Gamble (1996).
65   Antoninus Aurelius, M. (c.1900) *The Meditations of the Emperor Marcus Aurelius Antoninus*. Long, G. (trans.). London & Glasgow: Collins' Clear-Type Press. pp. 97–98.
66   Ibid.
67   Ward, S.C. (2015) 'The Role of the Arts in Society' In: Fleming, M., Bresler, L. & O'Toole, J. (eds.) *The Routledge International Handbook of the Arts and Education*. Abingdon: Routledge. pp. 106–121.
68   Ward, S.C. (2010) *Understanding Creative Partnerships: An Examination of Policy and Practice*. Doctoral Thesis, Durham University.

69 Adorno, T.W. & Horkheimer, M. (2010) *The Dialectic of Enlightenment.* Cumming, J. (trans.). London: Verso. p. 6.
70 Ibid.
71 Ibid: 6.
72 Friedman, M. in Enteman (1993: 46).
73 Ibid.
74 Ward, S.C., Bagley, C., Lumby, J., Woods, P., Hamilton, T. & Roberts, A. (2015) 'School Leadership for Equity: Lessons from the Literature' *International Journal of Inclusive Education, 19* (4), pp. 333–346.
75 Ibid.
76 Macleavy, J. (2010) 'Remaking the Welfare State: From Safety Net to Trampoline' In: Birch, K. & V. Mykhnenko, V. (eds.) *The Rise and Fall of Neoliberalism.* London: Zed Books. pp. 133–150.
77 Ward, S.C., Bagley, C., Lumby, J., Hamilton, T., Woods, P. & Roberts, A. (2016) 'What is "Policy" and What is "Policy Response"? An Illustrative Study of the Implementation of the Leadership Standards for Social Justice in Scotland' *Educational Management Administration & Leadership, 44* (1), pp. 43–56.
78 Ibid: 49.
79 Raffo, C. & Gunter, H. (2008: 398) 'Leading Schools to Promote Social Inclusion: Developing a Conceptual Framework for Analysing Research, Policy and Practice' *Journal of Education Policy, 23* (4), pp. 397–414.
80 Ibid.
81 Ward et al (2015: 337).
82 Jay (1967: 125).

4   Rational choice

Antony and Cleopatra

Introduction

In *The Constitution of Liberty*, Hayek postulated that governments' rationalist planning can never be truly effective or efficient as such planning is dependent upon imperfect information.[1] Far better, he claimed, for society to be ordered through the expression of individuals' free choice via the market mechanism. Ostensibly, this choice is rational, in that it furthers the interests of the individual and leads naturally to what Adam Smith described as a 'harmony of interests'.[2] As mentioned in Chapter 1, Hayek's theory of spontaneous order, or equilibrium, was challenged by James M. Buchanan, who believed that efficiency should be engineered, rather than left to chance.[3] Buchanan's Public Choice theory thus makes a case for the 'positive arm' of the state to act as both 'policeman' and 'participant' in the social realm.[4] Consistent with Buchanan's philosophy, English higher education reform has been presented as a movement towards efficiency, engineered by government but operationally dependent upon students' exercise of rational choice in the education marketplace.[5] This chapter will argue that, in reality, the marketisation of higher education is a movement towards negative liberty, defined after Isaiah Berlin as unrestricted choice.[6] This unrestricted choice is evident in Shakespeare's *Antony and Cleopatra*, where the relationship between rationality and sensibility is explored through the dramatisation of a series of political decisions of far-reaching consequence. By offering a reading of English higher education reform through *Antony and Cleopatra*, this chapter considers how negative liberty, far from functioning as a panacea to inefficiency, risks undermining human connectivity and debasing our relationships.

Antony and Cleopatra

Antony and Cleopatra depicts the political struggle between the Triumvirate of Rome, consisting of Lepidus, Governor of Africa, Octavius Caesar, Governor of Europe, and Mark Antony, Governor of Asia. Through a series of battles and betrayals, Octavius Caesar emerges as the sole ruler of the Roman territories and master of Egypt. As the title suggests, the play focuses primarily on the relationship between the Triumvir Antony and the Queen of Egypt, Cleopatra, and culminates in their spectacular suicides. Within this drama, the beauty of love is mixed so darkly with its powers of destruction that a straightforward celebration of love is not possible, and Antony's military collapse is shown to result from his failure to master his infatuation in the face of Caesar's pragmatism. By depicting a political stratagem that is fatally bound up with sex, Shakespeare shows the danger of allowing affairs of the heart to divert us from practical matters, such as political and economic advancement. The 'breathless haste'[7] of the play hurtles us towards the conclusion that Antony and Cleopatra have brought defeat upon themselves through their wild and hedonistic behaviour, yet at the very moment when we might feel satisfaction at the triumph of stability, represented by Rome, over debauchery, represented by Egypt, we feel instead sadness at the loss of this 'pair so famous' (5.2.350). Shakespeare, having appeared to be sweeping us towards catharsis at the defeat of chaos, collapses our certainty that this defeat is welcome. Towards the climax of the play we witness a moving scene between Antony and his follower Eros, whom Antony has freed from slavery. Eros is, of course, symbolic of unfettered love and desire. When Antony commands Eros to kill him he refuses, and falls upon his sword. First Eros, then Antony and finally Cleopatra commit suicide when faced with the prospect of life (or death) on Caesar's terms. Eros, Antony and Cleopatra 'connect person to world'[8] in the complex manner described by Martha Nussbaum, and Caesar's victory is won at the cost of their disconnection through self-annihilation. Having pursued a course of rampant self-interest, Caesar ends the play on his own – the sole surviving Triumvir – standing in a mausoleum built to honour the memory of the dead.

What does this wonderful story tell us? Caesar makes choices that appear to be logical, and consequently he is hailed as an Emperor. Antony and Cleopatra make choices that appear to be illogical, and consequently they forfeit their power and the lands they possess. We might conclude, therefore, that good things flow from rational choices, and bad things flow from irrational choices. But this cannot be the right way to read Shakespeare's work here, because Antony and Cleopatra are clearly ruined by the fact that their "choices" are *beyond* their rational control, and are not of their "choosing" at all. It is romantic love, heady and irresistible, that makes Antony turn around his ships at Actium and follow Cleopatra to his doom; it is the deep and mysterious bond of friendship that prompts Eros to kill himself rather than take Antony's life, and it is the love of self, coquettish and perhaps absurd, that makes Cleopatra commit suicide rather than face the prospect of being paraded through Rome as Caesar's exotic trophy. All of these decisions are bound up with a sensibility that is rejected by Caesar. Unable to win over his "irrational" opponents, he watches as his discipline results in them, one by one, embracing death in preference to life under the heel of Caesar. When thinking about English higher education reform, perhaps the most interesting way to understand *Antony and Cleopatra* is to consider how, within this drama, the imposition of one set of values crowds out another set of values that we may admire. Caesar's pursuit of self-interest and efficiency compromises, and thus drives out, Antony's passionate connection of 'person to world'.[9] It is to this idea that I would like to return, after looking next at the UK Coalition government's higher education policy for England (please note, higher education is a devolved matter in Scotland, Wales and Northern Ireland so *Students at the Heart of the System* is a White Paper for England only).

The White Paper: *Students at the Heart of the System*

After the dramatic splendour of *Antony and Cleopatra*, the Coalition's White Paper on Higher Education, *Students at the Heart of the System*[10] appears very drab. The 'system' it proposes to implement is immediately recognisable as the market system: the government makes clear its intention to establish a 'more market-based approach'[11] to university education, with students viewed as 'consumers',[12] and the Higher Education Funding Council for England (HEFCE) 'taking on a major new role as a consumer champion'.[13] The publication of league tables is fundamental to the commodification of education, as they inform consumers' choice of educational provider by providing information about pupils' academic performance (*see Chapter 5*). Critics of marketisation largely reject the neo-classical economic assumption that it is possible for information to be perfect and costless, and argue that league tables have impacted negatively on learning and teaching, as discussed in Chapter 1. For example, James Marshall argues that the pursuit of perfection (the highest league table position) has subsumed educational ideals, such as personal autonomy and emancipation, under the demands of efficiency,[14] and Alan Hudson claims that commodification has transformed English schooling into a 'shallow and fetid pool'.[15] As noted in Chapter 1, the problem of "teaching to the test" was officially recognised in 2008 by a House of Commons Select Committee, which found that teachers in both primary and secondary schools were impairing pupils' understanding and enjoyment of subjects by focussing on routine exercises and exam preparation.[16] The Coalition's decision to use the title *Students at the Heart of the System* for its White Paper on higher education thus shows a flagrant disregard for those academics who have identified a link between the imposition of the market system and the stifling of individuals' creativity and intellectual freedom, traits that we might associate with "being a student". The idea that we might want to place our university students at the 'heart' of this system is therefore disturbing.

The champions of this dysfunctional mission identify themselves in the introduction to the White Paper as the Secretary of State for Business, Innovation and Skills, Vince Cable, and the Minister for Universities and Science, David Willetts. Walter Cohen describes Octavius Caesar as 'a bureaucrat of the future';[17] perhaps we may think of Cable and Willetts as the "heirs to Caesar". It is, therefore, worth comparing some of Caesar's rhetoric with his latter-day counterparts. Towards the end of the play, a follower of Antony informs Caesar that Antony is dead. Instead of celebrating outright his victory over Antony, Caesar laments the passing of his former comrade, proclaiming:

> The breaking of so great a thing should make
> A greater crack. The round world
> Should have shook lions into civil streets,

And citizens to their dens. The death of Antony
Is not a single doom; in the name lay
A moi'ty of the world.

(5.1.13–19)

Caesar thus acknowledges that the imposition of his values has wiped out some-thing else that held value. In contrast, in their introduction to the White Paper, Cable and Willetts declare:

> The Coalition will reform the financing of higher education, promote a bet-ter student experience and foster social mobility. Our overall goal is a sector that is freed to respond in new ways to the needs of students.[18]

Cable and Willetts do not appear to share Caesar's scruples: they are striving to create a 'better student experience', conceived in terms of market performance and measured through student satisfaction surveys, with scant regard for the experience that they are displacing. They want higher education to be 'freed', but don't tell us *how* or *why* unreformed universities are shackled to practices that prevent them from responding to the needs of students. Unlike Caesar, Cable and Willetts appear to be charging ahead with reform without pausing to reflect on what it is that they may be eradicating in the process.

Clearly, Cable and Willetts are in the grip of the ideology of the market, hence their wish to turn students into 'consumers'. In general, the desire to commodify education is underpinned by rational choice theory, or the belief that individuals are 'rational, self-interested, have a stable set of internally consistent preferences, and wish to maximise their own happiness (or "utility") given their constraints, such as the amount of time or money that they have'.[19] The Enlightenment economist Adam Smith postulated that competitive market forces will always guide self-interest into socially useful activities, and that government intervention is not necessary because 'a competitive market system naturally leads to a *harmony of interests*'.[20] On the basis of this claim, the Coalition government is attempting to create a market system of education that appeals to the self-interest of the individual student, which it identifies as economic self-advancement through the cultivation of employability. The government therefore pledges to publish a longitudinal data-set that will reveal the differing economic returns of educational courses by tracking 'typical students through their journey from school, through higher education, into a career'.[21]

Following the maxim that the pursuit of self-interest makes everyone better off, the government goes on to state that:

> Better informed students will take their custom to the places offering good value for money. In this way, excellent teaching will be placed back at the heart of every student's university experience.[22]

The idea that 'excellent teaching' should reflect the preferences of students, rather than be determined by some kind of academic elite, seems democratic, and owes much to Isaiah Berlin's theory of positive and negative liberty, which he first put forward in 1958. According to Berlin, positive liberty is despotic, as it is assumes there is one true answer to human problems, while negative liberty gives individuals the freedom to do what they want.[23] The market model ensures that individuals' wants are satisfied without the imposition of ideological constraints: students are free to decide what constitutes excellent teaching, and to purchase education according to their preferences. Berlin cautioned against the adoption of negative liberty as a totalising theory, which would of course make it indistinguishable from positive liberty, but his advice fell upon deaf ears. Governments in the UK and elsewhere appear to share Buchanan's conviction that we should oblige everyone to be free agents in a free market, hence the desire of Cable and Willetts to create a higher education sector that is 'freed to respond in new ways' to students' needs.[24] Their apparent disregard for the justification of policy, mentioned previously, perhaps indicates the extent to which politicians have been indoctrinated to accept without question the need to embrace a concept of negative liberty that was, ironically, intended to free us from indoctrination. In this regard, Cable and Willetts are very poor successors to Caesar. Ultimately, Shakespeare's Caesar is worthy of at least some of our respect because, unlike politicians today, he does not blindly follow dogma, but instead reflects upon his strategy and understands entirely the implications of his actions: Caesar may desire 'total construction',[25] but he recognises that each civilization has a particular life of its own that may be destroyed in the process.

The more we compare the Coalition's plans for higher education with *Antony and Cleopatra*, the grimmer those plans appear. Caesar promises that 'the time of universal peace is near' (4.6.4), and this assertion anticipates the *pax Romana* instituted by Caesar throughout the empire.[26] When considering this 'peace', it is worth remembering the words of the Caledonian chieftain, Calgacus, in his speech (or the speech that is put into his mouth by the historian Tacitus) to his clansmen about the greed and arrogance of Rome:

> *Auferre, trucidare, rapere, falsis nominibus imperium; atque, ubi solitudinem faciunt, pacem appellant.*
> Plunder, slaughter, theft: this under the misnomer of Empire. They make a wasteland and call it peace.
>
> (Tacitus, *Agricola* 30.6)

A variation on the translation of Tacitus appears in Byron's poem, *Bride of Abydos* (1813, Canto 2, stanza 20): 'He makes a solitude, and calls it – peace!' The idea of solitude is captured by Shakespeare at the close of *Antony and Cleopatra* when messy, noisy human connectivity is displaced by the relative calm of Caesar's lonely triumph, and Shakespeare, Tacitus and Byron prompt us in different ways to reflect on the desirability of peace that is achieved through the eradication of other people. While the peace that Caesar brings is welcome, up to a point, the same can hardly be said for the marketisation that neoliberalism is bringing us. Not so long ago our political leaders promised to shield us from the extremes of the market system. In their manifesto on the Third Way, UK Prime Minister Tony Blair and German Chancellor Gerhard Schroeder reassured voters that 'We support a market economy, not a market society'.[27] Somewhere along the way the pretence has been dropped. Reading *Students at the Heart of the System*, it seems obvious that our politicians do in fact intend to create a 'market society'. Our unease over this phenomenon no doubt explains the popularity of Michael Sandel's book, *What Money Can't Buy: The Moral Limits of Markets*.[28] According to Sandel, 'we corrupt a good, an activity, or a social practice whenever we treat it according to a lower norm than is appropriate to it'.[29] Through the act of commodification, we impose a cash value on goods that should be beyond financial measurement and in so doing we debase them. Using examples such as the trade in babies, human blood and access to elite universities, Sandel demonstrates how marketisation corrodes social bonds and demeans us as human beings.

Not surprisingly, given its promotion of the market system, *Students at the Heart of the System* contains worrying evidence of the potential for the kind of corruption and debasement identified by Sandel. Under the heading 'Improving the student experience', the government promises to 'introduce a risk-based quality regime' that 'gives power to students to hold universities to account'.[30] The students are empowered – via the publication of their evaluation of teaching – to punish and shame universities that somehow fail to meet their expectations. Yet, equally, the universities are encouraged to monitor and report on students to prevent them from 'supporting or turning to terrorism'.[31] It is hard to imagine how granting staff and students the ability to exercise tyranny over one another will produce the 'harmony of interests' envisioned by Adam Smith. Indeed, there is compelling evidence that the market system increases inequality and lowers social cohesion, which in turn reduces political participation, weakens people's monitoring of government activity, decreases government efficiency and increases corruption.[32] Far from creating harmony, marketisation produces winners and losers, and debases democratic societies by promoting 'the world of master and slave' as described by Albert Camus.[33]

Today in England, "slavery" might be said to take the form of economic bondage. Fundamental to *Students at the Heart of the System* is the introduction of a new fees regime that obliges students to take out enormous loans from the State to pay for their higher education. Buried deep within the White Paper is a fearsome promise. Under the heading 'Improving the management of a growing student loan book' it states:

> The Government has tasked Rothschild to lead a feasibility study to assess the options for how to monetise the loan book. The feasibility study is considering a full range of options, including retaining the loans on the government's books, selling them outright to financial investors, or selling loans to one or more regulated companies set up to manage the loans.[34]

Young people in England are being encouraged to take on a lifetime of debt that cannot be shed through bankruptcy, and which may be sold on to unknown 'financial investors', at the very moment when our bankers and financiers have been exposed as 'sophisticated scam merchants'.[35] Referring to Plato's story of Gyges the shepherd, Fintan O'Toole describes how bankers today are corrupted by the 'ring of invisibility' that prevents most of society from seeing what they are doing. Consequently, O'Toole claims, 'They enjoy virtual impunity for acts that harm other people and society as a whole'.[36] The Coalition government's White Paper on higher education threatens to bind students through debt to invisible financiers who are not democratically accountable to the public, and thereby risks compromising democracy through the creation of opaque power structures based on debt.

The implications of changes to how we provide English higher education are more than financial. As we have seen, Shakespeare's characters in *Antony and Cleopatra* are attached to one another through emotions that are neither "useful" nor "rational", but which nevertheless give meaning to their lives, and his play therefore prompts us to reflect on how the market system risks undermining human connectivity through the values it fosters in education. In her book, *Not for Profit: Why Democracy Needs the Humanities*, Nussbaum discusses how marketisation has placed the pursuit of self-interest – in the form of credentials for employment – at the centre of education, and thereby undermined the concept of education for democracy. Through the promotion of rampant individualism, Nussbaum argues, the market system of education is condemning us to emotional isolation by diminishing our capacity 'to approach another person as a soul, rather than as a mere useful instrument or an obstacle to one's own plans'.[37] It seems that by fixating on market values we are 'forgetting about the soul, about what it is for thought to open out of the soul and connect person to world in a rich, subtle, and complicated manner'.[38] Nussbaum shows us that we may "succeed" by scrambling over others to secure a place at an elite university and land a top job, but ultimately our victory is hollow if, along the way, we have forgotten how to connect with others.

Through *Antony and Cleopatra*, Shakespeare reminds us that our choices are, at times, beyond our rational control, and he thereby shows us the folly of imagining that we might successfully organise our lives around "rational choice theory" and build a stable society based on market values. Negative liberty, described after Berlin as unrestricted choice, does not automatically lead to the creation of an orderly society ruled only by self-interest, as the pursuit of self-interest debases and unravels our relationships. As stated previously, Caesar's pursuit of self-interest and efficiency drives out Antony's exhilarating embrace of connectivity, and Shakespeare seems to recognise in principle what Sandel identifies for us today – that market values crowd out all other values and lead to the disconnection described by Nussbaum. Sadly, it seems that the UK government has failed to recognise that by prioritising the transmission of "skills for employability" it is emptying education of other values. Discussing funding arrangement it states:

> There is of course far more to higher education than financial benefit. It can transform people's lives for the better as their intellectual horizons are

broadened. Nevertheless, graduates do, on average, earn more than non-graduates and their higher education is one reason for this.[39]

With the word 'Nevertheless', the government turns its back upon the conception of education as anything more than a means to enhance economic self-advancement through employability, and thereby narrows and diminishes the significance of learning in the same way that Shakespeare's Caesar narrows the Triumvirate, and what it means to be 'Roman', down to himself. There is, perhaps, a danger that Jean-François Lyotard's assertion that we must 'be operational (that is, commensurable) or disappear'[40] will prove correct, and values that lie outside the accepted range of values within education, which are increasingly defined in terms of individuals' employability and institutional performance maximisation, will be abandoned. Staff and students who are unwilling to 'bend to the forces'[41] of marketisation may simply disappear from higher education.

When considering the possibility that our current policy makers are the 'heirs to Caesar', it is obvious that it is not possible to make a straightforward comparison of *Antony and Cleopatra* and *Students at the Heart of the System*. As stated earlier, Shakespeare exposes our frailties without resolving them, and instead of catharsis in *Antony and Cleopatra* we are given only a deeper awareness of what our fears, desires and insecurities may be. Consequently, our response to the fall of Antony and the triumph of Caesar is ambivalent. When Caesar and Antony talk about patching up quarrels and excuses in Act 2.2, they seem to capture the sense that the Triumvirate is a patchwork quilt of people and ideas, straining at the seams, and it is perhaps the complexity of these ideas that makes it so difficult for audiences to align themselves completely with either Antony or Caesar. It is perhaps the *lack* of ideas, or genuine discussion, evident in *Students at the Heart of the System* that makes it hard to reconcile this White Paper with Shakespeare's play. Instead of weighing up the pros and cons of different approaches to higher education, the government asserts the market approach as though it were the non-negotiable "common sense" position, and thereby demonstrates a kind of unreflective "knowingness" in which everything is held to be self-evidently true. Interestingly, Shakespeare takes pains to resist any possibility of "knowingness" in *Antony and Cleopatra*. Our understanding of the characters' motives is deliberately limited by the scarcity of soliloquy, and occasionally individual characters, such as Ventidius and Silius, blur into one another. Cohen observes that in this play Shakespeare 'makes no distinction between public and private because nothing is private',[42] and all of these effects combine to produce a sense that *Antony and Cleopatra* is not a drama of individuals but of forces in nature that have no private, inner space. I would argue that the reason that a straightforward analogy between Caesar and the architects of the Coalition's White Paper on higher education is not possible is because the government's market ideology lies *outside* the divide between the two types of nature that Shakespeare depicts in *Antony and Cleopatra*, discussed below.

Apollonian individuation and Dionysian unity

Friedrich Nietzsche suggests that Ancient Greek tragedy owed its dramatic nature to the pull between two opposing forces in human nature: Apollonian composure and individuation, associated with sculpture, and the turbulent Dionysian joy of unity, associated with music.[43] Nietzsche's theory would seem to find expression in *Antony and Cleopatra*, where Antony and his lover Cleopatra are the central figures of hedonistic pleasure, while Caesar and his sister Octavia are the central figures of measured restraint. From the first scene onwards, Shakespeare builds up symbolic representations of the Dionysian and the Apollonian types of nature by linking Antony and Cleopatra with images of water and music, and Caesar and Octavia with images of dryness and sculpture. Thus Enobarbus' description of Cleopatra's arrival in Cilicia on her barge forms a dramatic contrast with Octavia's arid arrival in Rome, and the water-borne party on Pompey's boat highlights the difference between the drunken Antony and the sober Caesar, who refuses to 'wash' his brain (2.7.93). At the lowest point of their fall, Shakespeare depicts a subtle shift in Antony and Cleopatra from Dionysian debauchers to exemplars of Apollonian nobility through an exchange of the symbols of water and stone (see, for example Cleopatra's 'I have nothing / Of woman in me: now from head to foot / I am marble-constant', 5.2.237–9), and the previously dry Caesar is reduced to weeping upon the death of Antony, calling it news 'to wash the eyes of kings' (5.1.28). By merging attributes at the close of the play, Shakespeare offers us hope that, while the imposition of Caesar's values may crowd out other values we may admire, these values are marginalised, rather than totally eradicated. This marginalisation is given greater significance by the fact that Shakespeare raises, and rejects, the possibility of eradicating *both* the Apollonian and the Dionysian in this play. Following the drunken banquet at sea, Menas urges Pompey to cut loose the boat and murder both Caesar and Antony. While Shakespeare shows us the limitations of a world in which the Dionysian is marginalised, he does not show us a world in which the dual aspects of human nature are killed off, as advocated by Menas as the most rational course of action for Pompey. Nietzsche described rationality as 'a dangerous, life-undermining power'[44] and explored what Shakespeare touches upon, and recoils from, in *Antony and Cleopatra*: the possibility of a world in which both Apollonian composure and Dionysian joy have been eradicated. Arguably, the world of market values, expressed through *Students at the Heart of the System*, is that world, and it is perhaps for this reason that the analogy between Caesar and the authors of the White Paper breaks down. The Coalition's White Paper is antithetical to the dual aspects of our nature as both reflective and reckless, and exists in a bureaucratic dead zone, making the government's utterances on education policy as equally unlike Caesar's measured political judgement as they are Antony's wild love-making.

Conclusion

Slavoj Žižek discusses how the global dimension of capitalism can only be 'formulated at the level of truth-without-meaning',[45] and Sandel and Nussbaum both eloquently express how the imposition of market values is withering our capacity for human interaction and weakening our ability to find meaning in our lives. The model of higher education put forward in *Students at the Heart of the System*, and the rationale for the "freedom" it purports to offer universities and students, is informed neither by Apollonian decorum nor Dionysian joy, but by the rejection of the possibility of any kind of human splendour. Žižek suggests there is a 'grain of truth'[46] in the worldview espoused by Ayn Rand, a contemporary of Isaiah Berlin and one of the early architects of market fundamentalism. Yet Rand's vision of money as the 'root of all good'[47] and her assertion that financial transactions, rather than human interaction, offer our surest protection from tyranny, rests upon the same faith in our capacity for rational choice put forward by Berlin, which Shakespeare exposes as unreliable. In *Antony and Cleopatra*, Shakespeare's characters respond to one another in a manner that, while not always rational or productive, speaks of a depth of human connectivity that is denied by market fundamentalism, and has therefore been written out of English higher education policy.

Perhaps the greatest lesson that Shakespeare offers us in *Antony and Cleopatra* consists not in what he tells us, but what he chooses to pass over in silence: the possibility of denying the full expression of human nature is raised in *Antony and Cleopatra*, but is never realised. The Coalition's decision to create a market system in higher education is a decision to assert the non-existence of our capacity for both critical reflection and spontaneous action, and this assertion has far-reaching implications for higher education in England and beyond. Of course, we know that Pompey did *not* murder Caesar and Antony, and Shakespeare would have needed to deviate wildly from his historical source material to depict this crime, yet the fact that he depicted its *contemplation* should give us pause to think about making real what Shakespeare, in fiction, depicts as a proposal that is swiftly dismissed.

Notes

1 Hayek, F.A. (2011) *The Constitution of Liberty: The Definite Edition*. Hamowy, R. (ed.). Chicago: The University of Chicago Press.
2 Hill, R. & Myatt, T. (2010) *The Economics Anti-textbook: A Critical Thinker's Guide to Microeconomics*. London: Zed Books. p. 13.
3 Buchanan, J. (1975) *The Limits of Liberty: Between Anarchy and Leviathan*. Chicago: The University of Chicago Press.
4 Olssen, M. & Peters, M.A. (2005: 319) 'Neoliberalism, Higher Education and the Knowledge Economy: From the Free Market to Knowledge Capitalism' *Journal of Education Policy, 20* (3), pp. 313–345.
5 BIS (2011) *Higher Education: Students at the Heart of the System*. London: HMSO.
6 Berlin, I. (2007) *Isaiah Berlin: Liberty*. Hardy, H. (ed.). Oxford: Oxford University Press.
7 Smeaton, O. (1922) *Shakespeare: His Life and Work*. London: J.M. Dent & Sons. p. 444.
8 Nussbaum, M. (2010) *Not for Profit: Why Democracy Needs the Humanities*. Princeton, NJ: Princeton University Press. p. 6.
9 Nussbaum (2010: 6).
10 BIS (2011) *Higher Education: Students at the Heart of the System*. London: HMSO.
11 Ibid: 73, §6.31.

12 Ibid: 68, §6.10.
13 Ibid: 2.
14 Marshall, J.D. (1999) 'Performativity: Lyotard and Foucault through Searle and Austin' *Studies in Philosophy and Education*, 18, pp. 309–317.
15 Hudson, A. (2004: 18) 'Educating the People' In: Hayes, D. (ed.) *The RoutledgeFalmer Guide to Key Debates in Education*. Abingdon: RoutledgeFalmer. pp. 18–22.
16 The Children, Schools and Families Committee, House of Commons (2008) *Testing and Assessment. Third Report of Session 2007–8*. London: HMSO.
17 Cohen, W. (1997: 2620) 'Antony and Cleopatra' In: Greenblatt, S. (ed.) *The Norton Shakespeare*. New York: W.W. Norton. pp. 2619–2627.
18 BIS (2011: 3).
19 Hill & Myatt (2010: 9).
20 Ibid: 13 (italics in original).
21 BIS (2011: 32 §2.21).
22 Ibid: 32, §2.24.
23 Berlin, I. (2007) 'Two Concepts of Liberty' In: Hardy, H. (ed.) *Isaiah Berlin: Liberty*. Oxford: Oxford University Press. pp. 166–217.
24 BIS (2011: 3).
25 Hayek (2011: 132).
26 Cohen (1997).
27 Blair, T. & Schroeder, G. (1998) *Europe: The Third Way/Die Neue Mitte*. Available online at: http://library.fes.de/pdf-files/bueros/suedafrika/02828.pdf [Accessed 30th March 2016].
28 Sandel, M. (2012) *What Money Can't Buy: The Moral Limits of Markets*. London: Allen Lane.
29 Ibid: 46.
30 BIS (2011: 10, §25).
31 Ibid: 35, §3.12.
32 Hill & Myatt (2010: 21).
33 Camus, A. (2009: 627) ' "Creation and Revolution" from *The Rebel*' In: Harrison, C. & Wood, P. (eds.) *Art in Theory: 1900–2000*. Oxford: Blackwell Publishing. pp. 626–629.
34 BIS (2011: 24, §1.42).
35 O'Toole, F. (2012) 'In Corrupt Systems, Decent People Have Two Options: Conform or Be Crushed' *The Observer* 1st July, p. 29.
36 Ibid.
37 Nussbaum (2010: 6).
38 Ibid.
39 BIS (2011: 17, §1.15).
40 Lyotard, J.-F. (2005) *The Postmodern Condition: A Report on Knowledge*. Manchester: Manchester University Press. p. xxiv.
41 Blake, N., Smeyers, P., Smith, R. & Standish, P. (2000) *Education in an Age of Nihilism*. London: RoutledgeFalmer. p. 173.
42 Cohen (1997: 2621).
43 Nietzsche, F. (1995) *The Birth of Tragedy*. Fadiman, C.P. (trans.). New York: Dover Thrift Editions.
44 Nietzsche, F. (2009) *Ecce Homo*. Large, D. (trans.). Oxford: Oxford University Press. p. 46.
45 Žižek, S. (2011) *Living in the End Times*. London: Verso. p. 365.
46 Ibid: 290.
47 Ibid.

5 Commodification

King Lear

Introduction

The preceding chapters of this book have considered the ideological basis of the market society, and this chapter asks if marketised relations are *inevitable*. Inspired by Lars Engle's assertion that Shakespeare viewed 'social interaction as an economy'[1] and treated 'truth, knowledge, and certainty as relatively stable goods in such an economy rather than gateways out of it',[2] this chapter offers a critique of commodification through a reading of *King Lear*, and in so doing asks if it is possible to exit the market mechanism. For Colin Burrow, *King Lear* is an enactment of Seneca's Stoical vision of a society 'founded on a complex system of exchanges between emotions and material goods';[3] a system that, if broken down, 'could unleash the uncontrolled rage of a would-be tyrant who can control nothing, not even his own self'.[4] According to this reading of the play, Lear's madness is born from the breakdown of the system of exchanges between master and servant, parent and child – a phenomenon underpinned by Seneca's theory on gratitude and the debt we owe those from whom we have derived emotional and material benefit. For David Hawkes, however, Lear's error is to assume that subjective phenomena can be quantified in the same way that material goods can be quantified, as, he says, to view love in quantitative terms is to alter its very nature and degrade it to the level of exchange-value.[5] By assigning "cash value" to his daughters' expression of gratitude for the paternal care he has shown them, Lear embarks upon a calamitous journey into the market system, making *King Lear* a useful lens through which to consider education's direction of travel.

King Lear

Lear, King of Britain, gathers his family in his palace for the purpose of conferring on 'younger strengths' (1.1.42) the governance of his kingdom, and asks his three daughters Goneril, Regan and Cordelia, 'Which of you shall we say doth love us most, / That we our largest bounty may extend / Where nature doth with merit challenge?' (1.1.53–55) Commodification is the process through which phenomena are evaluated according to their exchange value in the context of trade,[6] and by declaring that he will exchange his land for his daughters' expression of love, Lear commodifies both space and affection: a double violation of what Hawkes identifies as the feudal theory of economics. According to Hawkes, in ancient times the term 'economics' referred to 'the science of utility'[7] or subjective use-value, while chrematistics was the 'science of exchange'.[8] In the modern era, economic science has consumed chrematistics, and Hawkes argues that in blurring the distinction between use-value and exchange-value we have relinquished an 'essentially qualitative outlook',[9] which sees things in terms of their essences, and embraced instead a quantitative approach, which evaluates things 'according their relations to other things'[10] – a phenomenon explored most presciently in *King Lear*. By commodifying his kingdom, Lear disregards the medieval conception of the use-value of communal space, and also violates the traditional injunction against honouring one's parents above honouring the word of God, expounded in works such as Thomas Becon's *The Catechism*.[11] In so doing, Lear transforms God-given nature, both physical and spiritual, into exchange-value. While Goneril and Regan are happy to indulge their father's desire for extravagant protestations of love in exchange for land, his youngest daughter, Cordelia, will not permit her love to be commodified. When asked what she might say to obtain a third of Britain 'more opulent' (1.1.88) than her sisters, she replies, 'Nothing, my lord' (1.1.89), and when pressed she declares in line with Becon, 'I love your Majesty / According to my bond, no more nor less' (1.1.94–95). Cordelia's response enrages Lear, who refuses to give her land in return for her paltry tribute, and so divides her portion of his commodified love between her sisters.

Questions such as 'Is my love for my child as useful as my house?' strike us as inappropriate, yet commodification gives rise to such uncomfortable questions, as Lear swiftly discovers. Having resolved to spend alternate months with Goneril and Regan, accompanied by one hundred knights, Lear begins his sojourn with his eldest daughter, Goneril, who soon expresses her impatience with her father's retinue of 'disorder'd', 'debosh'd' and 'bold' men (1.4.248). Lear refuses to comply with Goneril's request to dismiss fifty of his followers, and applies to Regan for greater hospitality. Rather than refute Goneril, Regan asks, 'What need you five and twenty? Ten? Or five? / To follow in a house where twice so many / Have a command to tend you? (2.4.260–262) In the face of Regan's cold logic, Lear reverts to the language of non-commodified relations, where value is not found in equivalence but in essence:

> O, reason not the need! Our basest beggars
> Are in the poorest thing superfluous.
> Allow not nature more than nature needs,
> Man's life is cheap as beast's. Thou are a lady:
> If only to go warm were gorgeous,
> Why, nature needs not what thou gorgeous wear'st,
> Which scarcely keeps thee warm.
>
> (2.4.263–269)

This conversion to non-marketised relations comes too late, as Lear's market transaction has rendered him, in Goneril's words, an 'Idle old man, / That still would manage those authorities / That he hath given away' (1.3.17–19). Although Lear now recognises the folly of abandoning Cordelia, he persists in the belief that 'I am a man / More sinn'd against than sinning' (3.2.59–60); a sentiment that betrays a lingering belief that it is his eldest daughters' villainy, rather than his employment of the market mechanism, that has caused the psychic storm he must now endure. It is not until the conclusion of the drama, when Lear and his would-be saviour Cordelia are captured by the armies of Goneril and Regan, that Lear fully revokes marketised relations. In a scene that might be described as the ill-matched bookend to his fateful divestment of his kingdom, Lear now displays no interest in the exchange value of love or even liberty, but instead welcomes prison as a means to enclose everything he holds most dear. Joyfully, Lear says to Cordelia, 'Come, let's away to prison: / We two alone will sing like birds i' th'cage' (5.3.8–9). Cordelia's death by hanging ends Lear's dream of happy captivity, and in his sorrow he reverts to the language of equivalence, saying 'Why should a dog, a horse, a rat, have life / And thou no breath at all?' (5.3.308–309). In weighing the value of Cordelia's life against the animals invoked in his earlier dialogue with Regan, Lear raises the troubling prospect that man's life *is* as 'cheap as beast's' (2.4.266).

Equivalence and movement

As we have seen, *King Lear* closes with the contemplation of equivalence, and the theme of commensurability is established at the outset of the play when the Earls of Kent and Gloucester discuss which son-in-law is most favoured by Lear. Gloucester remarks that their 'equalities are so / weighed that curiosity in neither can make choice / of either's moiety' (1.1.5–7); a refrain that is repeated in soliloquy by his illegitimate son Edmund, who finds equivalence between himself and his brother Edgar. Edmund believes that his 'dimensions are as well compact', his 'mind as generous' and his 'shape as true' (1.2.7–8) as Gloucester's legitimate son and heir, and on the basis of this evaluation declares, 'Well then, / Legitimate Edgar, I must have your land' (1.2.15–16). For Matthew Smith[12], Lear represents the 'disintegrating feudal state', while Edmund represents the 'nascent Machiavellian state',[13] and by invoking the concept of moral flexibility in the pursuit of power, the Gloucester subplot provides a dark variation on the theme of commodification. Unlike Lear, whose bequests are born of a conscious identification of exchange-value, Gloucester's decision to disinherit Edgar is engineered by his duplicitous son Edmund. Already unsettled by Lear's bizarre division of his kingdom, Edmund's suggestion that Edgar is planning patricide prompts Gloucester to declare that, 'These late eclipses in the sun and moon portend no good to us' (1.2.112). In discerning a correspondence between human emotion and the cosmic order, or 'great chain of being',[14] Gloucester reveals that he is sympathetic to the Stoicism of Marcus Aurelius Antonius, who enjoins us to:

> Constantly regard the universe as one living being, having one substance and one soul; and observe how all things have reference to one perception, the

perception of this one living being; and how all things act with one movement; and how all things are the co-operating causes of all things which
exist; observe too the continuous spinning of the thread and the contexture
of the web.[15]

In soliloquy, Edmund ridicules his father's faith in astrology, saying, 'This is the
excellent foppery of the world, that when we are sick in fortune – often the
surfeits / of our own behaviour – we make guilty our disasters the sun, the moon,
and stars' (1.2.128–230). Edmund refuses to blame the heavens for his character, saying 'I should be that I / am, had the maidenliest star in the firmament
twinkled on my bastardising' (1.2.143–144). From this we may surmise that
Edmund subscribes to the twelfth-century canonists' definition of *jus naturale*
as a subjective force or ability characteristic of human beings,[16] which Larry Siedentop describes as 'free will or power',[17] and rejects the Stoics' definition of *jus
naturale* as 'the objective natural law' that pervades the universe.[18] For Edmund,
it seems, being equivalent to his brother means possessing his material wealth,
rather than sharing his ability to discern objective natural law. Under this worldview, the Stoics' "web of being" becomes a metaphor for the consumption of the
unwary, rather than universal connectivity.

Gloucester's contemplation of planetary movement underscores the theme of
transition within *King Lear*, and his mysticism is evocative of the Stoical belief
that 'The universe is transformation: life is opinion'.[19] For Marcus Aurelius, only
our subjective opinion has the power to perturb us, as things that are external to
us 'do not touch the soul':[20] living in a world of perpetual change, our universal
capacity for reason remains constant and enables us to interrogate the opinion
that forms within us. Marcus Aurelius believes that our 'intellectual part' must
be derived from 'some source',[21] as 'nothing comes out of that which is nothing,
as nothing also returns to non-existence'.[22] This supposition is reinterpreted by
those characters in *King Lear* who subscribe to the doctrine of marketisation. As
mentioned previously, 'Nothing' is Cordelia's response to her father's request
for tribute:

LEAR. . . . . what can you say to draw / A third more opulent than your sisters?
      Speak.
CORDELIA. Nothing.
LEAR. Nothing?
CORDELIA. Nothing.
LEAR. Nothing will come of nothing. Speak again.

(1.1.87–92)

In this dialogue, Cordelia uses 'nothing' to denote her non-participation in the
act of commodification, whereas for Lear 'nothing' is a unit of exchange. Lear's
Fool uses this concept of exchange-value to torment his master later in the play,
saying that Lear's exchange of land for love has rendered him 'an O / without a figure. I am better than thou are now: I / am a Fool, thou art nothing'

(1.4.198–200). As with Edmund's concept of equivalence, the Fool's concept of nothingness suggests the grim possibility of being reduced to zero in the market society through an unwise transaction, rather than the benign impossibility of the existence of phenomena external to the cosmic chain of being. While Edmund uses this "insight" to make rationally self-interested transactions that reduce his brother to a ragged wanderer on the heath, the Fool uses this same insight to alternately jibe his master and plead with him to renegotiate terms with his daughter and thus come in from the storm. In a tragically unhinged rendition of Cordelia's moral stance on commodification, Lear ignores the Fool's advice saying, 'No, I will be the pattern of all patience, I will say nothing' (3.2.37).

Change and continuity

In *King Lear*, the act of commodification is intended to yield the fruits of meliorism, defined by Colin Koopman as 'improvement, progress, and betterment',[23] and within the play there is a sustained tension between those characters who pursue change as a means to betterment and those who favour continuity. When considering the characters' readiness to favour change over continuity, it is perhaps helpful to reflect upon the Stoics' observation that the 'universe is either a confusion, and a mutual involution of things, and a dispersion; or it is unity and order and providence'.[24] For Marcus Aurelius, if the former is true then we may as well embrace death, while if the latter is true, 'I venerate, and I am firm, and I trust in him who governs'.[25] Arguably, Lear's steadfast companion Kent exemplifies the latter position, while the Machiavellian Edmund exemplifies the former. As though to underscore this division, Shakespeare depicts a storm in which the characters loosely associated with continuity wander outside in the rain, while the characters associated with change remain comfortably indoors. Much speculation has been made over the meaning of the storm in *King Lear*,[26] which might be read either as an example of the confusion of the universe or a "natural" revolt against the violation of natural and divine law, as seen in *Macbeth*. According to Leslie Thomson, the sound of thunder in Jacobean drama usually indicated that something supernatural was about to occur,[27] yet in *King Lear* it is desperate men who spill onto the stage with the onset of the tempest, rather than paranormal entities, and Shakespeare's reluctance to assure us that the universe is not a godless confusion has prompted critics to describe *King Lear* as his most pessimistic play.[28] However, for A.C. Bradley *King Lear* conveys the message that the only real thing in this world is 'the soul, with its courage, patience, devotion. And nothing outward can touch that'.[29] If Bradley is correct, then the conclusion of *King Lear* confirms the Stoics' belief that 'the universe is transformation; life is opinion' and that the soul cannot be harmed by things external to it. It is perhaps no coincidence that the survivors of this tragedy are Gloucester's non-Machiavellian son Edgar, the stalwart Kent, and Goneril's husband Albany, who questions his Machiavellian wife's faith in meliorism, remarking that 'Striving to better, oft we mar what's well' (1.4.353).

In contrast to the dichotomy of change and continuity depicted by Shakespeare, Hayek believed that social order emerges through an organic process of 'adaptive evolution',[30] which involves both change *and* continuity. According to Hayek:

> Those who believe that all useful institutions are deliberate contrivances and who cannot conceive of anything serving a human purpose that has not been consciously designed are almost of necessity enemies of freedom. For them freedom means chaos.[31]

For Hayek, freedom does *not* mean chaos, as the expression of free choice under the market mechanism yields social order. If we hold the classical view that "value" is fixed and discoverable through the exercise of reason, then we are likely to believe that order is the product of rational deliberation, rather than the unplanned outcome of market transactions, and that the search for equivalence, rather than essence, will result in the kind of chaos depicted in *King Lear*. If, however, we agree with Hayek that the value of an item or behaviour is relative rather than absolute, we may discover its customary utility by observing its exchange-value in a given context. Crucially, for Hayek, the market mechanism does not require us to have fundamental understanding of phenomena, just sufficient knowledge of traditional values to optimise our choices. The by-products of the pursuit of self-interest – or the "aggregate of utility" – are social order and 'useful institutions'. Hayek quotes from J. Ortega y Gasset, who says 'Order is not pressure imposed upon society from without, but an equilibrium that is set up from within'.[32] It seems that for Hayek, equilibrium is established through the market mechanism.

As stated previously, the concept of "nothing" as a unit of exchange is entwined with the act of commodification in *King Lear*, and critics of the market mechanism have identified scarcity as a key factor in the establishment of the alleged equilibrium of the market society. In *Money and the Age of Shakespeare*, Scott Cutler Shershow claims that early societies were grounded in practices of mutual gift-giving, rather than the management of 'scarce resources' as in modern capitalist societies,[33] and claims that the practices of gift exchange and market exchange coexisted in Shakespeare's time, with the latter model becoming preeminent more recently. According to George Bataille, these models of exchange are based upon competing ideas about the cosmos. Using the analogy of the sun, which produces heat and light without asking for anything in return, Bataille argues that the 'general' (gift-exchange) economy considers the unlimited bounty of the universe, while the 'restricted' (market-exchange) economy considers the limited resources of the individual.[34] Beliefs about the general and the restricted economy are related to our sense of what Shershow describes as our 'being-in-common':[35] if I believe that the universe is abundant and contains more than one individual can have, think or say, then the recognition of the limits of my personal accumulation becomes the basis of my access to the 'open-ended limitlessness whose name is *community*'.[36] Conversely, if I believe that goods are scarce and that there might not be enough to go around, then the restriction of my individual access to goods becomes the basis of my pursuit of self-interest in the free market, and the resultant 'aggregate of selfishness'[37] perpetuates the fear of scarcity. Seen in this light, the equilibrium of the market society is predicated upon the disavowal of the collective gift of nature's bounty and the acceptance of the Fool's fearful supposition that it is possible for an individual to have, and to be, "nothing".

The commodification of education

Neoliberal mechanisms for improving the commodity value of educational outcomes are associated with the operation of the market, namely competition (parental choice), transparency (performance indicators) and comparison (league tables).[38] The purpose of commodification is to facilitate pupils' market participation, rather than to ensure equality of life outcome, and the fear of having and being "nothing" is thus fundamental to the neoliberal model of education and underpins the anxiety over the accruement of credentials discussed in Chapter 1. Andrew Wilkins argues that the act of commodification has obliged parents, in 'their role as consumers',[39] to adjust 'their attitudes and values to fit with an instrumental rationality that privileges competitiveness and autonomy'[40] rather than equity and solidarity. Although not as punitive as the measures taken to cajole educators into compliance with the neoliberal project (*see Chapter 2*), Wilkins is critical of the services offered by specialists to help parents make school choices. According to Wilkins, the purpose of such government assistance is to develop an 'ethical framework'[41] in education in which the 'pursuit of competitive familial advantage is naturalized as both legitimate and necessary'[42] and in which the Machiavellian display of 'acquisitive, calculating behaviour and zero-sum thinking' is considered to be healthy.[43]

As well as being alarmed by the promotion of behaviour which is depicted as morally debasing in both *Macbeth* and *King Lear*, we might share A.O. Karpov's concern that the commodification of education works in the interests of the elite by obfuscating the role that social status plays in employability so that the inequitable sharing of risk in the market society is hidden from view. As noted by Karpov, 'The educational supermarket offers a readymade assortment of services and goods for the "consuming" personality, an array that has been created and decided on *by someone*'.[44] The question of who benefits from the commodification of education is, of course, the crux of the matter for many writers on this topic. As noted by Stephen Ball, 'In fetishising commodities, we are denying the primacy of human relationships in the production of value, in effect erasing the social'.[45] Presumably, this erasure is not problematic for parents and pupils who lean towards Edmund's pragmatic rejection of his father's Stoical view of the universe, and under this analysis we might expect pupils who, like Cordelia, value the primacy of human relationships to fare most badly in the market society. This is not, however, necessarily the case: as noted by Hayek, the market mechanism is ethically neutral and does not differentiate between those who love it and those who loathe it. The pursuit of self-interest in the market society does *not* guarantee material success, irrespective of one's ideology, as the outcome of market transactions is primarily determined by one's economic, rather than ideological, investment. The economist Thomas Piketty devoted fifteen years to the study of the historical dynamics of wealth and income, and reached the troubling conclusion that the market economy based on private property has consolidated wealth in hands of a tiny elite, and that global investment in education has done little to abate this tendency.[46] We might respond to this finding by citing Hayek's argument that liberty means the exercise of choice, rather than the accruement of property, yet Piketty argues that liberty is threatened by the accumulation of capital by the entrepreneur, who becomes 'a rentier, more and more dominant over those who own nothing but their labor'.[47] Piketty demonstrates how those who have capital gain more capital to chilling effect, so that 'The past devours the future'.[48] It seems that the pursuit of credentials for employment is a rigged contest, with prizes awarded to pupils whose parents already possess those prizes and may therefore distribute them as they wish. In light of Piketty's analysis it is perhaps wise for us to share Karpov's scepticism over the social justice of commodification, which purports to make everyone enjoy the same happy "shopping experience".

At the beginning of the twenty-first century, Ball lamented the international 'paradigm convergence'[49] that has underpinned the widespread commodification of education, and the apparent lack of resistance to neoliberal marketisation and its colonisation of education is, perhaps, the outcome of contemporary philosophers' reluctance to endorse the concept of unity that is the counterweight to commodification in *King Lear*. For example, in *The Postmodern Condition*, published in 1979, Jean-François Lyotard claimed that in the wake of the terror of the nineteenth and twentieth centuries, 'Consensus has become an outmoded and suspect value'[50] and identified what he describes as a 'decline of narratives of legitimation':[51]

> In the context of delegitimation, universities and the institutions of higher learning are called upon to create skills, and no longer ideals – so many doctors, so many teachers in a given discipline, so many engineers, so many administrators, etc. The transmission of knowledge is no longer designed to train an elite capable of guiding the nation towards its emancipation, but to supply the system with players capable of acceptably fulfilling their roles at the pragmatic posts required by its institutions.[52]

In Lyotard's analysis we may glimpse the nascent interest in "what works" in education: shorn of any esoteric dimension, education becomes a vehicle for meliorism, which is construed in economic terms as employability. Sadie Plant's analysis of *The Postmodern Condition* illustrates the futility of an ideological position that challenges the possibility of making legitimate truth claims: if reality is constructed through discourse, then it becomes impossible to disentangle "our" perspective from the power relations that give rise to our sense of self.[53] In lieu of the Stoics' conception of the soul untouched by things external to it, we have the conception of the self as an arrangement of external effects. Plant describes

how this idea was pursued by Deleuze and Guattari, who 'abandoned all vestiges
of progress and surrendered to a world populated only by an ever more anarchic
chaos of desires';[54] a sensibility not unlike that displayed by the Machiavellian
Edmund in *King Lear*. Indeed, Gloucester's poignant epigraph, 'As flies to wan-
ton boys, are we to th'gods, / They kill us for their sport' (4.1.36–37) seems an
apt description of Edmund and his fatuous murder of Cordelia. However much
we share Lyotard's concern over the totalitarian 'terror' of the nineteenth and
twentieth centuries,[55] his clarion call, 'Let us wage war on totality'[56] is not perhaps the response to market relations suggested by *King Lear*.

"What works"

In his analysis of Shakespeare's art, Lars Engle defines pragmatism as 'the substitution of dynamic economies for fixed structures',[57] and claims that pragmatism
has been attacked as a theory that colludes with free-market capitalism. In pragmatism's defence, Engle asserts that this philosophy 'is antithetical to the idea
that one form of economic organization, the so-called free market, is natural and
therefore fundamental to optimal social forms',[58] taking as its object instead the
interrogation of the 'complex relations between modes of economic organization
and the ways people are shaped by them'.[59] However, Hayek's tendency to invoke
pragmatism when describing the ethical neutrality of the market mechanism (*see
Chapter 3*) makes it difficult to disentangle the philosophy espoused by Engle
from the neoliberal project, and indeed Engle's assertion that 'pragmatists focus
on what works, on what can be made visible'[60] was echoed by UK Prime Minister
Tony Blair in his famous declaration that 'What counts is what works'.[61] Nowhere
is the neoliberal interest in "what works" more apparent than in the field of educational research. For example, in 2002 the What Works Clearinghouse (WWC) was
established by the Institute of Education Sciences (IES) at the US Department of
Education, to provide 'educators, policymakers, researchers, and the public with
a central and trusted source of scientific evidence about "what works" in education'.[62] Similarly, in 2013 the Education Endowment Foundation and the Sutton
Trust were jointly designated by the UK government as the What Works centre
'for improving education outcomes for school-aged children'.[63]

The opposite of "what works" is, of course, "what doesn't work", making it difficult to challenge the philosophical practice of pragmatism, defined by Koopman
as meliorism: 'the attitude of improvement, progress, and betterment'.[64] However,
in his critique of the commodification of education, Michael Apple claims that the
benefits of identifying the "best" education are not evenly distributed,[65] meaning
that research into "what works" cannot be considered to be unequivocally good.
Indeed, in light of the analysis of Machiavellianism in Chapter 3, the pursuit of
"what works" might even be described as pernicious, and researchers who seek to
discover "what works" in schools and colleges might be likened to a 'midwife',[66]
hired to bring into existence a workforce willing to bear risk in the market society. In
a foreshadowing of Tony Blair's "what works" maxim, David Hargreaves claimed
that in 'education we too need evidence about what works with whom under what

conditions and with what effects'.[67] During the 1990s, educational researchers in the UK were at the cutting edge of research into the multiple measures of pupil outcomes, which included such things as locus of control; attendance; delinquency; behavioural problems; attitudes to school; self-esteem; attitudes to school subjects; academic outcomes; gender; parental socio-economic status; parental education; parental ethnicity; age and race.[68] To its supporters, school effectiveness research (SER) seemed to offer the potential to maximise educational performance by modelling within-school complexities. To its critics, however, SER provided the mechanism for comparative data that consumers need to make markets work, and numerous educationalists expressed their concern over the observation that schools that were attracting the "right" kind of parents with the "right" kind of pupils were effectively blocking the enrolment of disadvantaged pupils by driving up property prices in the catchment area.[69] Thus, while common sense says that SER is good because it enhances school performance, in reality the benefits of identifying "what works" are not evenly distributed.[70]

In 2015, the US Department of Education published a report, *Usages of Practices Promoted by School Improvement Grants.*[71] The School Improvements Grants (SIG) programme aims to 'support the implementation of school intervention models in low performing schools'[72] by promoting 'the usage of instructional practices that have the potential to increase academic rigor and achievement of students'.[73] This objective involves the identification of 'teacher and principal effectiveness criteria',[74] and it is therefore apparent that the quest for "what works" is bound up with what Ball describes as the 'terror of performativity'[75] (*see Chapter 3*). Although Ball's use of this phrase is an obvious nod to Lyotard's philosophy, it seems unlikely that such "terrorism" might be combatted by educators' countermoves in a postmodern "language game". Instead of acting as a buffer to commodification, the counter discourses to neoliberalism are drowning in what Ignacio Ramonet describes as the 'liquid' penetration of the market into every corner of society,[76] enabling the naturalisation of the commodification of education to go virtually unchallenged.

'Which of you shall we say doth love us most?' (*King Lear*, 1.1.53)

If, like Lear's daughters, we are willing to meet the terms of commodification, then we must be prepared to exchange something in the marketplace. In the English higher education sector (and to a large extent the US higher education sector), the student exchanges money for access to the potential to accrue credentials for his/her employment. But what do state-funded school children, their parents, teachers or indeed, educational researchers, exchange in the education marketplace? To answer this question, it is perhaps helpful to consider the purported function of neoliberalism. According to David Harvey, neoliberalism is:

> . . . a theory of political economic practices that proposes that human well-being can best be advanced by liberating individual entrepreneurial freedom

and skills within an institutional framework characterized by strong private property rights, free markets, and free trade. The role of the state is to create and preserve an institutional framework appropriate for such practices . . . Furthermore, if markets do not exist (in areas such as land, water, education, health care, social security, or environmental pollution) then they must be created, by state action if necessary.[77]

From this we might surmise that state education functioned outside the market mechanism prior to the adoption of neoliberalism, meaning that its commodification is a philosophical preference, rather than a practical necessity. In light of *King Lear*, we might define commodification as an ideological act that obliges us to reject the belief that education is a gift that is bequeathed by one generation to the next, and to embrace instead the idea that I must give my elders something in return for this bounty. This "something" is, quite simply, the acceptance that something must always be given for something: as put by Lear, 'Nothing will come of nothing' (1.1.92). The commodification of education is, then, an assault upon the concept of the abundant universe; a concept that Shershow believes leads us towards community and which undermines the operation of the market mechanism by denying the concept of scarcity that fuels the pursuit of self-interest.

As discussed in Chapter 1, the commodification of education has gone hand-in-glove with political scaremongering over the blighted life chances of pupils who have failed to "purchase" employability in the form of credentials, and in Chapter 2, a similar pressure was noted with regard to school teachers who have become figurative debtors in their classrooms' market transactions and evicted from the profession. Underpinning these stories of deficit and loss is the dread of the Fool's "nothingness", and it is perhaps disheartening that so many educational researchers have chosen to fuel this fear by making protestations of love for "what works", rather than adopting Cordelia's stance of non-compliance, irrespective of the difficulties identified above. As I have noted elsewhere, the 2010 report on the Research Excellence Framework (REF) made it clear to UK academics that *everything* can be bought and sold as a commodity, and that what cannot be sold, either figuratively as a strategy for improving classroom practice or literally as a ticket-only arts event, is irrelevant.[78] To date, this celebration of commodification has excited little protest, and UK academics are perhaps more likely to attend their institutions' research impact workshops and form grant application cells than to follow Cordelia into figurative exile. This response is, of course, understandable: academics are not rendered immune to the fear of "nothingness", couched in terms of career stagnation and redundancy, simply because we are professional thinkers.

Conclusion

This chapter began by asking if marketised relations are inevitable. Lear's act of commodification is shown to be ruinous, but *not* inevitable: had he chosen to listen to Kent's injunction to employ his reason to acknowledge Cordelia's intrinsic goodness, there would have been no tragedy. In *King Lear*, Shakespeare appears to acknowledge the coexistence of market-exchange and gift-exchange, and through Gloucester's astrological ruminations he suggests that our preference for either form of exchange is likely to be informed by our belief system, as theorised by Bataille. Shakespeare's art does not indicate, however, that this observation alone will render us immune from neoliberal ideology. In *Measure for Measure* Shakespeare exposes the difficulty of mastering our belief systems, and the sense of godlessness that permeates *King Lear* seems to prompt us to suppose that we will receive little in the way of transcendental assistance to guide our choices. With neither extrinsic nor intrinsic forces to assist us, we must make our lonely way in this world – a supposition expressed gently by Edgar to his blinded and broken father: 'Men must endure / Their going hence, even as their coming hither: / Ripeness is all' (5.2.9–11). Arguably, *King Lear* serves to warn us that our endurance is tested most arduously when we place our hopes for betterment in the pragmatic identification of exchange-value and its attendant fear of "nothingness." The rejection of the grand narratives of legitimation that occurred in the latter part of the twentieth century, as identified by Lyotard, has made it difficult for academics to make truth claims that might challenge neoliberalism's hold over the political imagination. In addition, the market mechanism's own disavowal of ideology has ensured that the academic critique of commodification is no more than a rubber bullet, unable to pierce the hide of capital. Choices were made in the past, as in Lear's kingdom, that have led to the triumph of Machiavellian instrumentality in modern democracies, but going forward we may still ask, 'Is commodification inevitable'? Piketty's analysis of capitalism implies that, unless we are prepared to remove the "rentier entrepreneur" from the pedestal of hero and to disavow the mythology of risk in the market society, the answer will continue to be 'Yes'.

Notes

1 Engle, L. (1993) *Shakespearean Pragmatism: Market of His Time*. Chicago: The University of Chicago Press. p. 3.
2 Ibid.
3 Burrow, C. (2013) *Shakespeare and Classical Antiquity*. Oxford: Oxford University Press. p. 199.
4 Ibid.
5 Hawkes, D. (2015) *Shakespeare and Economic Theory*. London: Bloomsbury Publishing Plc. p. 123.
6 Watson, G.L. & J. Kopachevsky, J.P. (1994: 645) 'Interpretations of Tourism as Commodity' *Annals of Tourism Research*, 20 (3), pp. 643–660.
7 Hawkes (2015: 16).
8 Ibid.
9 Ibid.
10 Ibid.
11 Danby, J.F. (1949) *Shakespeare's Doctrine of Nature: A Study of King Lear*. London: Faber and Faber.

12 Smith, M. (2015: 6) ' "Crack Nature's Molds": Reasoned Madness and Evolution in *King Lear' Utopia and Political Theology*, 5 (2), pp. 1–22. doi:10.15291/sic/2.5.lc.1.
13 Ibid.
14 Ibid.
15 Antonius, M.A. (c.1900) *The Meditations of the Emperor Marcus Aurelius Antonius*. Long, G. (trans.). London & Glasgow: Collins' Clear-Type Press. p. 134.
16 Tierney, B. in Siedentop, L. (2015) *Inventing the Individual: The Origins of Western Liberalism*. London: Penguin. p. 357.
17 Siedentop (2015: 357).
18 Tierney in Siedentop (2015: 357).
19 Antonius, M.A. (c.1900: 123).
20 Ibid.
21 Ibid: 124.
22 Ibid: 123–124.
23 Koopman, C. (2009) *Pragmatism as Transition: Historicity and Hope in James, Dewey, and Rorty*. New York: Columbia University Press. p. 17.
24 Antonius, M.A. (c.1900: 159).
25 Ibid: 160.
26 Egan, G. (2006) *Green Shakespeare: From Ecopolitics to Ecocriticism*. Abingdon: Routledge.
27 Thomson, L. (1999) 'The Meaning of *Thunder and Lightning*: Stage Directions and Audience Expectations' *Early Theatre*, 2, pp. 11–24.
28 Bradley, A.C. (1987) 'From *Shakespearean Tragedy*' In: Fraser, R. (ed.) *William Shakespeare: The Tragedy of King Lear*. New York, NY: Signet Classic. pp. 225–242.
29 Bradley (1987: 242).
30 Hayek, F.A. (2011) *The Constitution of Liberty: The Definitive Edition*. Hamowy, R. (ed.). Chicago: The University of Chicago Press. p. 115.
31 Ibid: 122.
32 Gasset in Hayek (2011: 215).
33 Shershow, S.C. (2003: 100) 'Work and the Gift: Notes toward an Investigation' In: Woodbridge, L. (ed.) *Money and the Age of Shakespeare*. Basingstoke: Palgrave Macmillan, pp. 97–112.
34 Bataille, G. in Shershow (2003).
35 Shershow (2003: 109).
36 Ibid. Italics in original.
37 Ibid.
38 Elliot, J. & Doherty, P. (2001) 'Restructuring Educational Research for the "Third Way"?' In: Fielding, M. (ed.) *Taking Education Really Seriously: Four Years Hard Labour*. London: RoutledgeFalmer. pp. 209–221.
39 Wilkins, A. (2012: 71) 'School Choice and the Commodification of Education: A Visual Approach to School Brochures and Websites' *Critical Social Policy February*, 32, pp. 69–86.
40 Ibid.
41 Ibid: 72.
42 Ibid.
43 Ibid.
44 Karpov, A.O. (2013: 78) 'The Commodification of Education' *Russian Education and Society*, 55 (5), pp. 75–90. Italics in original.
45 Ball, S.J. (2004) 'Education for Sale! The Commodification of Everything?' King's Annual Education Lecture. University of London. p. 4.
46 Piketty, T. (2014) *Capital in the Twenty-First Century*. Goldhammer, A. (trans.). London: The Belknap Press of Harvard University.
47 Ibid: 571.

48 Ibid.
49 Ball, S.J. (2001: 48) 'Labour, Learning and the Economy: A "Policy Sociology" Perspective' In: Fielding, M. (ed.) *Taking Education Really Seriously: Four Years Hard Labour.* London: RoutledgeFalmer. pp. 45–56.
50 Lyotard, J.F. (2005) *The Postmodern Condition: A Report on Knowledge.* Bennington, G. & Massumi, B. (trans.). Manchester: Manchester University Press. p. 66.
51 Ibid: 65.
52 Ibid: 48.
53 Plant, S. (1997) *The Most Radical Gesture: The Situationist International in a Postmodern Age.* London: Routledge. p. 119.
54 Ibid: 122.
55 Lyotard (2005: 81).
56 Ibid: 82.
57 Engle (1993: 4).
58 Ibid: 5.
59 Ibid.
60 Ibid: 55.
61 Blair, T. (1997) *New Labour because Britain Deserves Better.* Available online at: http://www.politicsresources.net/area/uk/man/lab97.htm [Accessed 26th January 2016].
62 What Works Clearing House (2016) *Frequently Asked Questions.* Available online at: http://www.ies.ed.gov/ncee/wwc/Document.aspx?sid=15#wwc [Accessed 26th January 2016].
63 What Works Network (2016) Available online at: https://educationendowment foundation.org.uk/about/what-works-network/ [Accessed 26th January 2016].
64 Koopman (2009: 17).
65 Apple, M. (2006) 'Producing Inequalities: Neo-Liberalism, Neo-Conservatism, and the Politics of Educational Reform' In: Lauder, H., Brown, P., Dillabough, J.A. & Halsey, A.H. (eds.) *Education, Globalization & Social Change.* Oxford: Oxford University Press. pp. 468–489.
66 Ibid: 210.
67 Hargreaves, D.H. (1996) *Teaching as a Research-based Profession: Possibilities and Prospects.* London: Teacher Training Agency. p. 8.
68 Reynolds, D., Sammons, P., Stoll, L., Barber, M. & Hillman, J. (1996) 'School Effectiveness and School Improvement in the United Kingdom' *School Effectiveness and School Improvement, 7* (2), pp. 133–158.
69 Ryan, J. (2012) *Struggling for Inclusion: Educational Leadership in a Neoliberal World.* Charlotte, NC: Information Age Publishing, Inc.
70 Ward, S.C. (2010) *Understanding Creative Partnerships: An Examination of Policy and Practice.* Doctoral Thesis, Durham University.
71 Dragoset, L., James Burdumy, S., Hallgren, K., Perez-Johnson, I., Herrmann, M., Tuttle, C., Angus, M.H., Herman, R., Murray, M., Tanenbaum, C., and Graczewski, C. (2015). *Usage of Practices Promoted by School Improvement Grants* (NCEE 2015-4019). Washington, DC: National Center for Education Evaluation and Regional Assistance, Institute of Education Sciences, U.S. Department of Education.
72 Ibid: 1.
73 Ibid: 22.
74 Ibid: 28.
75 Ball, S. (2003: 215) 'The Teacher's Soul and the Terrors of Performativity' *Journal of Education Policy, 18* (2), pp. 215–228.
76 Ramonet, I. (2008) 'Chapter 1: Introduction' In: Brouillette, R. (Director) *Encirclement: Neo-liberalism Ensnares Democracy.* Québec, Canada: HDCam (shot in 16mm), B&W, 2008, 160 minutes.

77 Harvey, D. (2005) *A Brief History of Neoliberalism.* Oxford: Oxford University Press. p. 2.

78 Ward, S.C. (2014: 80) 'Education and the "New Totalitarianism": How Standards for Reporting on Empirical Studies of Education Limit the Scope of Academic Research and Communication' In: Smeyers P. & Depaepe M. (eds.) *Educational Research: Material Culture and Its Representation.* Dordrecht: Springer. pp. 71–85.

6 Knowledge

The Tempest

Introduction

In his analysis of Julien Benda's 1927 thesis on the 'treason of the intellectuals', Stephan Collini reminds us of the deep concern once shared by many over the philosophy espoused by the 'fierce teachers of realism'[1] who had abandoned the quest to 'preach the love of an ideal, of something supra-temporal'.[2] Today, perhaps, this distrust of "fierce realism" seems quaint, and certainly by the 1970s educationalists such as Paul H. Hirst had come to doubt the future of education theory animated by the Stoics' conception of 'the harmonious, hierarchical scheme of knowledge'.[3] The classical belief that liberal education 'frees the mind to function according to its true nature',[4] rather than conditions the individual for employment, rested upon the notion that knowledge is the understanding of reality in the cosmic chain of being. In contrast, the nineteenth-century psychologist and pragmatist philosopher, William James, argued that it is a 'tremendously mistaken attitude'[5] to believe that our opinions can never be 're-interpretable or corrigible',[6] as our responsiveness to a hypothesis is not dependent upon its 'intrinsic properties',[7] but upon its relationship to our existing beliefs and our 'willingness to act'.[8] For pragmatists, intrinsic properties of phenomena may be fixed and amenable to discovery through empirical enquiry, but human responsiveness is always fluid. John Dewey's pragmatist account of education (*see Chapter 2*) was therefore founded on the rejection of the 'spectator conception of knowledge', in which knowledge is the 'mere beholding or viewing of reality'.[9]

Rather than attempt to debunk progressivism, twentieth-century exponents of liberal education acknowledged that society no longer subscribed to the 'metaphysical doctrine about reality'[10] that underpinned Seneca's belief that the pursuit of wisdom 'prepares the mind for the acquisition of moral values',[11] and sought instead to defend liberal education on the grounds that it is 'concerned directly with the development of the mind in rational knowledge, whatever form it freely takes'.[12] In this chapter I argue that this capitulation, while no doubt expedient, paved the way for the reification of "transferable skills" as the defining feature of neoliberal pedagogy, and helped legitimise the teaching of literary studies and the humanities as a means to cultivate the next generation of leaders[13] while fostering what Michael Bristol describes as 'loyalty to a hegemonic social and cultural dispensation'.[14]

Shakespeare's last solo-authored romance, *The Tempest*, is widely regarded as his 'retirement play'[15] in which he bids farewell to the stage, making its consideration a fitting way to end this book. Robert M. Adams defines the literary "romance" as a quest narrative in which the wanderer 'seeks a goal which, if only for the purposes of the tale, is accepted as ultimate',[16] and many critics have imagined that Prospero represents Shakespeare's intention to give up his art and repose near his daughter and son-in-law in Stratford-upon-Avon. In this scenario we, the audience, who have been instructed and entertained by Shakespeare's "magic", must give him leave to depart. Such speculation should, perhaps, be treated with caution. As noted by David Scott Kastan, it is impossible to determine Shakespeare's religious convictions through an examination of his art,[17] and it is perhaps no less difficult to determine his views on the nature of the artist's knowledge. Nevertheless, *The Tempest* has been described by Arthur F. Kinney as a 'play of education'[18] due to the characters' frequent discussion of learning. Arguably, the defining feature of this quest narrative is Prospero's knowledge of magic and the role that it plays in the attainment of an ultimate goal, making this play a useful lens through which to view our ideas about the role of knowledge in education today.

The Tempest

The Tempest is unusual amongst Shakespeare's plays in featuring a protracted explication of its backstory, which centres around two themes related to knowledge: first, Prospero talks about his love of books, and how this love cost him his Dukedom of Milan; second, Prospero and his daughter Miranda talk about the difficulty of educating Caliban, the monstrous progeny of the dead witch Sycorax. Recalling his former life as the Duke of Milan, Prospero describes himself to Miranda as a man of 'dignity, and for the liberal arts / Without a parallel' (1.2.73–74). Prospero tells Miranda that in order to dedicate himself to his 'secret studies' (1.2.77) he gave the administration of Milan to his brother Antonio, who 'Being once perfected how to grant suits, / How to deny them, who t'advance and who / To trash for overtopping' (1.2. 79–81) overthrew and exiled his erudite but unworldly brother in the manner of a true Machiavel. Prospero describes scholasticism as 'the bettering of my mind' (1.2.90), and downplays the appeal of the political power that seduced Antonio, saying 'my library / Was dukedom large enough' (1.2.109–110). This assertion is repeated by Prospero when he recalls Gonzalo's kind assistance, saying, 'Knowing I loved my books, he furnished me / From mine own library with volumes that / I prize above my dukedom' (1.2.166–168). It seems that Prospero continues to rank psychic advancement more highly than Machiavellian self-advancement; a preference reminiscent of Aristotle's assertion that 'To seek utility everywhere is by no means the way of free men with a sense of their own dignity'.[19] For Aristotle, the paradigm of well-being is a life centred on theoretical contemplation, as illustrated by Prospero in Milan, while a life centred on political activity is worthwhile but inferior.[20] It is with some pride that Prospero reminds Miranda that he has shared with her the superior blessings of theoretical contemplation, saying 'Here in this island we arrived, and here / Have I, thy schoolmaster, made thee more profit / Than other princess' can that have more time / For vainer hours, and tutors not so careful' (1.2.171–174).

Prospero recalls that he did attempt to employ his knowledge to instruct the island's original inhabitant, Caliban, for his human betterment, and Miranda likewise reminisces about her endeavour to educate Caliban by teaching him to speak. Caliban acknowledges that Prospero taught him how 'To name the bigger light and how the less / That burn by day and night' (1.2.336–337) but is wholly unrepentant over his attempted rape of Miranda, which terminated all such humane instruction. Caliban has proved himself unworthy of liberal studies, defined by Seneca as 'the ones considered worthy of a free man',[21] and Miranda attributes Caliban's resistance to moral betterment to his essential condition as an 'Abhorred slave / Which any print of goodness wilt not take' (1.2.353–354). This sentiment is shared by Prospero, who later complains that Caliban is 'A devil, a born devil, on whose nature / Nurture can never stick; on whom my pains / Humanely taken – all, all lost, quite lost' (4.1.188–190). Prospero reminds Miranda that Caliban now 'does make our fire, / Fetch in our wood, and serves in offices / That profit us' (1.2.312-14). Caliban is thus positioned in the play by Miranda and Prospero as an example of what Aristotle describes as a 'natural slave'.[22] By performing acts of drudgery on behalf of the philosopher, he says, natural slaves contribute to the pursuit of the good life by helping their master achieve the state of *Eudaimonia*, or human flourishing. Natural slaves are themselves incapable of attaining *Eudaimonia*, no matter how much leisure they might be given, due to their incapacity to make reasoned judgements that are consistent with their conception of what it means to live well.[23] According to Aristotle, the natural slave enables the actualisation of a *system* of human flourishing, and the slave's own life is enhanced by what Malcolm Heath describes as 'participation in the master's deliberated ethical praxis'.[24] Although Shakespeare is careful to legitimise Caliban's subjugation through reference to his carnal desire for Miranda, Prospero's moral justification for making Caliban his slave is entirely consistent with his self-conceptualisation as a philosopher.

The 'masterless man'

Caliban's refusal to comply meekly with his master's demands might be read as a parody on the state-of-being that Paul Cefalu describes as 'masterlessness':[25] a phenomenon which haunted the imagination of Renaissance England. During the sixteenth century, increasing numbers of English landowners enclosed common land to expand their estates. No longer able to labour for themselves and unable to find alternate employment, the victims of enclosure wandered England in large bands begging for food, and their mobility in pursuit of sustenance alarmed the more affluent people who had caused this problem.[26] The emotional response to this displacement was complicated by the Reformation, which introduced the belief that the moral subject is produced through the dignity of labour, making unemployment sinful.[27] In 1598 and 1601 two Acts of Parliament, known together as the Elizabethan Poor Law, duly laid down requirements for pauper children to be placed, at the expense of their parish, as apprentices in the homes of masters until the age of 24 for males, and 21 for females.[28] These government-directed apprenticeships ensured that every common person (or Aristotelian natural slave) had a master and was tied to a geographic location. Seen in this light, Caliban's virtual imprisonment is consistent with the "moral" instruction meted out to the ordinary young men and women of Renaissance England.

In *The Tempest*, the social order mandated by the Poor Law is comically overturned when Prospero raises a storm that causes his brother's boat to be shipwrecked upon the island. Two royal servants, Stephano and Trinculo, find themselves washed upon the shore, where they encounter the disgruntled Caliban. Believing that their masters have drowned and that this island is their new home, Stephano and Trinculo are both repulsed and beguiled by Caliban's servility, and lend an ear to his proposal to share with them his knowledge of how to live upon the island in exchange for their agreement to murder Prospero. As noted by David Bevington, Caliban is 'beyond the reach of most instruction', yet 'his perceptions of natural beauty are remarkably sensitive'.[29] Although pitched to the drunken servants with deadly intent, Caliban's descriptions of the hidden bounty and subtle dangers of the island are indeed beautiful. Previously, Caliban belittled his linguistic instruction, saying to Miranda, 'You taught me language, and my profit on't / Is, I know how to curse. The red-plague rid you / For learning me your language' (1.2.364–366). Now Caliban discovers a new utility for his education, employing rhetoric to incite murder. Seneca quotes the saying, 'You've as many enemies as you've slaves',[30] and *The Tempest* seems to excite further anxiety by suggesting that education may *empower* your enemy. However, in keeping with the comic nature of the play, this supposition is swiftly dismissed through a skit on hunting. Aristotle proposes that 'hunting animals and subduing natural slaves are natural forms of acquisition'.[31] In *The Tempest*, a noise of hunters is heard and 'divers Spirits in shape of dogs and hounds' appear with 'Prospero and Ariel setting them on' (*stage directions, Act 4, scene 1*). This spectral pack proceeds to chase Caliban, Stephano and Trinculo off stage, thereby assuring us that Caliban and the drunken servants are the "natural acquisition" of men like Prospero, and the audience is invited to laugh at how easily such miscreants are vanquished. Shakespeare's willingness to find humour in the subjugation of natural slaves makes it difficult to support Kieran Ryan's conjecture that Shakespeare's characters are 'dramatized *from the perspective of* "common humanity"' that anticipates 'a genuinely human community no longer crippled by division and domination'.[32] It is perhaps more likely that Shakespeare was mirroring contemporary anxiety over the threat posed to civil society by "masterless" men, rather than anticipating a more equal society.

The 'magic womb'

In *Deschooling Society*, published in 1971, Ivan Illich describes compulsory education using language that calls to mind *The Tempest*. According to Illich, classroom attendance 'removes children from the everyday world of Western culture and plunges them into an environment far more primitive, magical and deadly serious'[33] where the 'rules of ordinary reality' are suspended.[34] The school, he says, psychically incarcerates children over many years in this 'sacred territory',[35] so that the classroom becomes a 'magic womb'.[36] As we have seen, Prospero regards the enchanted island as a schoolroom attended by his daughter Miranda and the delinquent Caliban, but the idea of the magic womb invoked by Illich is far older than Shakespeare's play. Through his discussion of Gaia, sleeping at Delphi '(from *delphys*, the womb)',[37] Illich invites us to consider the Ancient Greek origins of our ideas about education, which revolve around what John Burnet describes as 'the perennial problem':[38] should the end of education be culture, or should education 'fit us for the business of life'?[39] In the fifth century BC, the Sophists championed the latter ideal, promoting a fundamentally utilitarian model of education in which every branch of study is viewed as an instrument to increase 'power and efficiency'.[40] H.I. Marrou praises the Sophists for inventing the public lecture and being the first to recognise the value of the sciences, but describes their system of education as 'brazen in its cynical pragmatism'.[41] The Sophists sold their knowledge of Rhetoric to their pupils for their immediate and profitable use in statecraft, and by making practical life the highest object of education, Sophism came to be seen by critics such as Plato as the 'art of "getting off" by deception and flattery'.[42] Unlike the Sophist Protagoras, who declared that he did not know if the gods exist, and that 'it is a difficult question, and life is too short',[43] Plato advocated enquiry into difficult questions, not to 'store the memory with useful knowledge' but to create a 'mind capable of receiving intelligible truth'.[44] For Plato, this truth is divine – an idea supported and further developed by his pupil Aristotle. Aristotle claimed that we are always educated towards an end, defined as the completion of a process, and the ultimate end is happiness. For Aristotle, the gods are speculative, and the man who 'cultivates his intellect' is 'most dear to the gods',[45] as they 'rejoice in what is best and most akin to themselves'.[46] Because the man who is most loved by the gods is likely to be the happiest man, Aristotle surmises that 'the wise man will be the happiest'.[47] By the Hellenistic Age, says Marrou, the idea that education gives a man 'nobility of soul'[48] and invests him with 'a kind of sacred radiance'[49] had given classical education a 'dignity of a genuinely religious kind'.[50]

Mystical ideas about the power of education have continued into the modern era and underpin the concept of the 'magic womb' identified by Illich, but Aristotle's distain for practical activity has fallen out of favour more recently. According to Aristotle, 'It is, of course, obvious that we shall have to teach our children such useful knowledge as is indispensable for them; but it is equally plain that all useful knowledge is not suitable for education'.[51] In keeping with this ethos, Aristotle advocated basic instruction in music, but cautioned that pupils should not be educated to the level of a public performer as, he says, a man engaging in 'pursuits to please strangers would in many cases be regarded as following the occupation of a slave or a serf'.[52] Although patently ignored today, such advice made a deep impression on the upper classes of Renaissance Europe, as illustrated in 1529 by Thomas Lupset's composition, 'An Exhortation to Young Men', in which he prescribes a list of texts by Ancient Greek and Roman writers suitable for the instruction of gentlemen. For Lupset, philosophy is the antithesis of the 'mechanical . . . wage-earning occupations'[53] identified by Aristotle, which 'allow the mind no leisure' and thus 'drag it down to a lower level'.[54] Indeed, Lupset argues that 'These books shall lift you up from the clay of this earth and set you in a hill of high contemplation',[55] presumably far above the slaves and serfs.

In *The Tempest*, Prospero violates the injunction against practical activity and public performance and thus adopts the mantle of the natural slave which, as we have seen, is perhaps more proper to Caliban. Unwillingly relocated on the island, Prospero finds it necessary to transition from philosopher to practical magician. Once applied, Prospero's knowledge has a utility that parallels Antonio's exploitation of political guile in Milan, as it enables him to gain mastery over the monstrous Caliban and the ethereal Ariel in the same way that Antonio's statecraft 'new created / The creatures that were mine' (1.2.81–82) so that they willingly served a new master. Ignoring Aristotle's injunction against the use of professional skills for public delight, Prospero employs his art to entertain his island guests, commanding the spirits to perform exotic masques that fill the air with music. At the end of the play, Prospero is reinstated as the Duke of Milan and is free to return to a life of theoretical contemplation. Prospero duly vows to break his staff and drown his book of spells, thereby ridding himself of the tools of practical magic. He is likewise careful to avoid any display of political ambition unworthy of a speculative man, saying that upon his return to Milan, 'Every third thought shall be my grave' (5.1.312). No wonder, then, that so many critics have argued that Shakespeare, who could not afford to live the life of a 'wise man' as defined by Aristotle, modelled Prospero upon himself: it is only through retirement that the artist is granted manumission.

Dewey's response to 'spiritual culture'

As a quest narrative, *The Tempest* resembles Dewey's account of 'Education as Unfolding',[56] which he aligns with the classical tradition. Under this model of education, development is conceptualised as 'the unfolding of latent powers toward a definite goal . . . conceived of as a completion, – perfection',[57] rather than a 'continuous growing'.[58] In *The Tempest* this goal is the reinstatement of Prospero in his correct role as the Aristotelean 'wise man' of Milan. Shakespeare's play might therefore be described as an enactment of what Dewey calls the 'developmental doctrine' that 'speaks of the ideal and spiritual qualities of the principle which is unfolding'.[59] As discussed in Chapter 2, the Victorian poet Matthew Arnold promoted Hellenistic education as a means to cultivate the 'nobility of soul' alluded to by Marrou. However, Victorian exponents of liberal education seemed unable to explain *how* classical knowledge performs this feat, prompting philosophers such as Dewy to conclude that liberal education was akin to a religious cult. According to Dewey:

> The conception that growth and progress are just approximations to a final unchanging goal is the last infirmity of the mind in its transition from a static to a dynamic understanding of life.[60]

For Dewey, this 'dynamic understanding of life' is based upon the recognition that 'an individual can only live in the present'[61] and that the cultural products of the past are only useful insofar as they enable us to critically interrogate our present situation. According to Dewey, 'the true object of knowledge resides in the consequences of directed action',[62] making speculation relevant only when directed towards practical activity: the inversion of Aristotle's belief. Rejecting the idea that speculative activity is favoured by 'the gods', Dewey also rejected the idea that liberal education uplifts the soul. In *Democracy and Education*, published in 1916, Dewey asserted that:

> . . . the idea of perfecting an "inner" personality is a sure sign of social divisions. What is called inner is simply that which does not connect with others – which is not capable of free and full communication. What is termed spiritual culture has usually been futile, with something rotten about it, just because it has been conceived as a thing which a man might have internally – and therefore exclusively.[63]

Dewey challenged the morality of using classical knowledge as a marker of social status, and provided his own definition of slavery, not as something inherent to people who are incapable of attaining *Eudaimonia*, but as something that arises when people are 'engaged in activity which is socially serviceable, but whose service they do not understand and have no personal interest in'.[64] For Dewey and his followers, progressive education frees pupils from a life of servitude by developing their capacity for critical reflection, thereby helping them to question their social actions and live in fuller communion. In contrast, liberal education traps pupils in a 'sterile'[65] culture whose influences 'educate some into masters' and 'others into slaves',[66] and which serves these masters badly by fashioning 'manners fastidious rather than humane'.[67]

Constructivism

During the twentieth century, progressive educators' research into the cognitive processes at work when children learn developed into the theory of constructivism, which asserts that 'knowledge is always knowledge that a person constructs'.[68] For the constructivist, says Matthew Conduct, 'knowledge is not a true or accurate representation of an external reality, but a kind of organisation of concepts, expectations and abilities that enables successful coping with the world that we experience'.[69] Conduct points out that there is an equally strong tradition of trying to understand knowledge in terms of its correspondence to a world that is independent of the mind, and cautions that by favouring constructivist thinking in education we risk closing down debate about the nature of truth and knowledge. This concern is shared by D.C. Philips, who describes constructivism as a ' "powerful folktale" about the origins of human knowledge'[70] that rivals the classical 'magic womb' critiqued by Illich. Writing in the late 1990s, Philips contrasts Dewey's lack of interest in the 'internal politics of knowledge producing communities'[71] with more recent social-constructivist epistemologies, which stress that 'the knower cannot be conceived as being an artificially objectified and solitary individual isolated from a historical and sociocultural setting'.[72] The social-constructivist approach to knowledge ostensibly generates critical questioning that empowers marginalised groups, making it far more attractive than the subjugation of natural slaves depicted by Shakespeare in *The Tempest*. However, in the rush to prevent any single group claiming 'epistemic privilege',[73] it seems that we have supplanted the quest for knowledge with the expression of opinion. This move has resulted in the emergence of identity politics around such things as race, gender and sexuality – which many academics have welcomed – but the international endorsement of constructivism has also left many academics unsure about what constitutes knowledge and whether students' personal reflection should be the focus of assessment.[74] The consequent prevarication over truth claims has prompted Michael Devitt to describe constructivism as a dangerous ideology that 'attacks the immune system that saves us from silliness'.[75]

Knowledge in the market society

In her discussion of 'The end of knowledge',[76] Joanna Williams contrasts President John F. Kennedy's 1956 speech at Harvard University with the UK government's 1963 *Report of the Committee on Higher Education* (the *Robbins Report*). Kennedy, she says, talked of 'the advancement of knowledge and the dissemination of truth',[77] whereas the *Robbins Report* talked of education's ability to deliver economic benefits. At some point in the middle of the twentieth century, it seems, we let go of the idea of academic study as a route to transcendental truth and settled upon a more prosaic account of education. It is perhaps surprising that the neoliberal opponents of the permissive society presided over this collapse in certainty over truth claims, which escalated during the 1980s and peaked at the start of the twenty-first century in the vacuous accounts of higher education discussed in Chapter 4. Admittedly, in its infancy, neoliberal education policy did purport to champion traditional accounts of knowledge. Consider, for example, the 1988 Education Reform Act, which introduced the National Curriculum alongside the UK's performativity measures (*see Chapter 2*). For the first time in history, the UK government determined the content of what would be taught, set attainment targets for learning, and directed how performance would be assessed and reported.[78] Children were now legally obliged to study Shakespeare in what was seen by many as an appeal to Arnold's idea of "Hellenisation" through education. Indeed, Rhys Griffith claimed that the National Curriculum established a curriculum content and pedagogy 'familiar to the middle classes in the middle of the nineteenth century'.[79] This apparent triumph of humanism was, however, offset by the introduction of 'new vocationalism',[80] which ostensibly served the needs of industry by equipping pupils with generic employment skills such as time-management and computer literacy.[81] For example, the TVEI (the Technical and Vocational Educational Initiative), which was launched as a pilot scheme in 1983 and extended nationally in 1987, focussed on problem-solving in real world contexts and utilised child-centred methods that appealed to exponents of progressive education.[82] By introducing the National Curriculum *and* vocational education into English schools, the Conservatives under Margaret Thatcher were able to satisfy both the traditionalists who sought to preserve classical knowledge and the business leaders who demanded "employment ready" school leavers.[83]

The apparent fudge over the status of knowledge in the neoliberal curriculum appears to be incompatible with the rigorous ousting of progressive pedagogy discussed in Chapter 2. Why, we might ask, have politicians such as UK Prime Minister John Major boasted that 'The progressive theorists have had their say, and they have had their day',[84] and then mandated experiential learning? This mystery is cleared up if we recall the story of Thatcher throwing Hayek's *The Constitution of Liberty* on a table and declaring '*This* is what we believe'.[85] In this book, Hayek provides an explanation of the market mechanism that reveals the instrumental account of knowledge at the heart of the neoliberal project. According to Hayek, the market mechanism does not require us to have fundamental understanding of phenomena, just sufficient knowledge of *traditional values* to optimise our choices, and the by-products of the pursuit of self-interest are social order and useful institutions.[86] This perspective reflects Hayek's allegiance to what Philips describes as the 'secular religion'[87] of constructivism. According to Hayek:

> Man did not simply impose upon the world a pattern created by his mind. His mind is itself a system that constantly changes as a result of his endeavour to adapt himself to his surroundings. It would be an error to believe that, to achieve a higher civilization, we have merely to put into effect the ideas now guiding us. If we are to advance, we must leave room for a continuous revision of our present conceptions and ideals which will be necessitated by further experience.[88]

This 'continuous revision of our present conceptions and ideals' risks, of course, fostering the same instrumentality and slipperiness criticised by Plato and Aristotle in the fourth century BC, but this does not mean that neoliberals have disavowed the importance of knowledge. On the contrary, politicians such as the former UK Education Secretary Michael Gove have argued in favour of traditional pedagogy, describing the 'solace – and stimulus'[89] that working class children may find in the study of poetry. Like Hayek, however, Gove imagines that the end of such knowledge is non-transcendental 'social mobility',[90] couched in terms of enhanced earning potential through the accrument of skills and credentials for employment. In articulating this pragmatic goal, Gove references the cognitive theory underpinning constructivism:

> It is only when knowledge is secure in the long-term memory that it can be summoned up effortlessly and the working memory can be freed to deal with new and challenging tasks.[91]

The idea that knowledge is a means to an end, rather than an end in itself, is also expressed by the US's National Research Council in their report, *Education for Life and Work: Developing Transferable Knowledge and Skills in the 21st Century*, where they state:

> We view 21st century skills as knowledge that can be transferred or applied in new situations. Transferable knowledge includes content knowledge in a domain and knowledge of how, why, and when to apply this knowledge to answer questions and solve problems.[92]

Arguably, this instrumental approach to knowledge in the classroom has been lent credence by educators keen to preserve liberal education by flagging up its potential to cultivate the capacity for rational choice so highly prized by neoliberals. For example, Bristol argues that literary studies and the humanities have been used by conservatives in the USA to cultivate the next generation of leaders. According to Bristol, 'Shakespeare is the one absolutely unassailable icon for a cultural tradition',[93] yet the ideological basis of the contemporary discourse of leadership makes the appropriation of Shakespeare for its inculcation nonsensical. Despite Shakespeare's admonition of Machiavellian self-interest, his plays have been used to promote the free market concept of individuality through assessment activities that stress his unique genius, place emphasis on characterisation and require candidates to provide a 'personal response'.[94]

In what might be described as an affront to Aristotle's distain for Sophistry, Stephen Law claims that Aristotle's theory on the cultivation of good habits is 'particularly influential in today's 'character education' movement',[95] which he identifies as a focus of both the Democrat and Republican parties in the USA. According to Kevin Ryan, proponents of character education are keen to distance themselves from 'the faddism . . . of the Sixties and Seventies, when the emphasis was on process and teachers pretended that the culture has few moral principles or lessons to transmit'.[96] For neoliberals, these moral principles are grounded in economic theory about what constitutes a good citizen, defined as someone who is willing to bear risk in the market society. It seems, then, that the left-wing critique of cultural transmission (*see Chapter 2*) has been commandeered by exponents of the market society to cast doubt upon the status of knowledge as the *goal* of education. Instead, educators are encouraged to valorise students' subjective response to knowledge as a means of economic self-actualisation, which is conceptualised as the end of education. The result is perhaps most obvious in the domain of higher education: unsure about the ethics of the canon and wary of making imperialist assumptions about truth claims, academics have increasingly focussed on transferable skills for employability, such as group work, oral communication and time-management, as the "product" of higher education. Unable to sustain the rhetoric of education as a public good, many universities have been only too willing to position themselves as agents of the economy.[97]

Today, most of us are likely to agree with Dewey that it is socially divisive to offer speculative activity to "superior" children and practical activity to the children who will one day grow up to serve them. It is perhaps surprising, then, to recall that Dewey's challenge to the classical tradition was not warmly received by British socialists in the 1930s (*see Chapter 2*). To these socialists, pragmatism seemed to threaten the quasi-religious concept of knowledge as an end in itself: according to this way of thinking, liberation from the drudgery of alienated labour through education is meaningless if knowledge does not enable the working class scholar to attain the 'final unchanging goal'[98] of spiritual nobility, as postulated by Aristotle. Aristotle pitied those who have no ultimate goal: choosing things for the sake of something else, he says, they constantly ask 'what *use* is this?',[99] and cannot live a meaningful life as their 'desire is rendered futile by an infinite regress'.[100] For Seneca, a liberal education does not make a person good, but makes goodness possible by illuminating the goal that makes life meaningful: 'the pursuit of wisdom'.[101] By rejecting the idea that nature is 'a rational order or hierarchy of being'[102] in which everything has a fixed place discoverable through the exercise of reason, Dewey's progressive theory undermined the classical belief that knowledge forms a 'harmonious system' in which truth and goodness prevail.[103] In so doing, Dewey dismantled Aristotle's buffer to the instrumentality of Sophism, which might have shielded us from the instrumentality of neoliberalism. Today, instead of sharing Seneca's belief that it is not possible to admire education if its 'end is the making of money',[104] we are likely to believe that the purpose of education is to garner credentials for employment. US President Bill Clinton's famous political slogan, 'It's the economy, stupid',[105] has, it seems, become the mantra of our lives.

Conclusion

In *The Fountainhead*, published in 1943, Ayn Rand displays her contempt for 'conscious incompetence'.[106] By throwing off artistic convention, says her narrator, European architects freed themselves from 'arbitrary rules'.[107] However, instead of reaching new heights of creative expression, these architects began to disregard effort altogether and so made 'creative poverty'[108] into a system of 'mediocrity boastfully confessed'.[109] From this cautionary tale we may glimpse the neoliberals' hope for their socio-economic reforms, not as the destruction of tradition but as the freedom from the 'arbitrary rules' that constrain the heroic entrepreneur. The fact that things went awry for the architects in Rand's fiction might be described as prophetic, as today we bemoan the 'conscious incompetence' of modern democracies in which ordinary students clamour for credentials for employment in a global economic structure that patently favours the interests of the elite.[110] In his analysis of modernity versus postmodernity, Jürgen Habermas argues that critics of the permissive society blurred the relationship between societal modernisation and cultural development.[111] Failing to recognise the economic and social roots of the 'altered attitudes towards work, consumption, achievement, and leisure',[112] he says, these critics attributed the "social ills" of 'hedonism, the lack of social identification, the lack of obedience, narcissism, the withdrawal from status and achievement competition – to the domain of "culture" '.[113] In so doing, the critics of the permissive society turned our attention away from societal processes, which they could not explain, and projected the causes of social discontent 'onto the plane of a subversive culture and its advocates'.[114] Instead of linking arms with countercultural revolutionaries to resist the alienation of capitalism, exponents of neoliberalism sought salvation in the conceptual "purity" of laissez-faire capitalism, and vilified their opponents' attempts to collectivise risk as irrational, anti-heroic and totalitarian. From Habermas' analysis, it seems that Hayek, Rand, Friedman and others mistook the symptoms of social malaise for its cause.

The market utopia envisaged by the neoliberals as a corrective to the permissive society is, perhaps, of limited appeal, as it is predicated upon Hayek's notion of 'man *qua* man'[115] as the Machiavellian individualist. All utopias, of course, are bounded by the limits of their author's imagination. In *The Tempest*, Shakespeare includes a speech lifted almost word-for-word from Montaigne's essay 'Of the Caniballes'[116] in which the author claims to answer Plato's imaginary commonwealth.[117] In this speech, Gonzalo imagines a society in which there exists no division between liberally educated men and slaves, and thus no power imbalance between the likes of Prospero and Caliban. Gonzalo, however, perverts Montaigne's original speech through the insertion of the first-person pronoun to position himself as king of this utopia:

> I' th' commonwealth I would, by contraries,
> Execute all things; for no kind of traffic
> Would I admit; no name of magistrate;
> Letters should not be known; riches, poverty,
> And use of service, none; contract, succession,
> Bourn, bound of land, tilth, vineyard, none;
> No use of metal, corn, or wine, or oil;
> No occupation, all men idle, all;
> And women too, but innocent and pure;
> No sovereignty –
>
> (2.1.147–156)

At the word 'sovereignty' Gonzalo is interrupted by Sebastian and Antonio, who point out the absurdity of seeking to govern the free. Gonzalo's conceptual confusion is indicative of a tendency towards unconscious structural replication that is later and more fully expounded by Illich in *Deschooling Society*. According to this theory, our ideas about utopia are shaped by our experience of governance, making it difficult to find novel solutions to existing problems. Because Gonzalo serves a king, he cannot imagine a world without monarchs. To break this impasse, Illich borrows from *The Tempest* to describe the 'brave new world'[118] of deschooling, in which the institutions of learning that condition children's minds for the maintenance of existing social structures are closed down and individuals are instead issued vouchers for life-long voluntary learning. Illich's dream did not become reality, and arguably the extremity of his solution to unconscious structural replication made the neoliberals' rival pursuit of performativity appear modest in comparison.

Arnold's Victorian ideas about classical study complemented a political structure in which only a certain section of the male population had the vote, making a discourse of master and slave logical. Clearly, this model is not appropriate in modern democracies where adults enjoy universal suffrage. Arguably, the neoliberal project is an egalitarian attempt to marry elitism with pragmatism: the 'brave new world' ushered in by neoliberal reform has, after all, positioned traditional knowledge not as something that constrains us, but instead as a set of values that guides our expression of self-interest in the market mechanism. However, when viewed through the lens of Shakespeare's Renaissance humanism, these values are found wanting. In *Hamlet*, entrepreneurial risk-taking appears to be antithetical to the emotional life of the scholar; in *Measure for Measure* the methods used to transform the permissive society are oppressive rather than liberating; in *Macbeth* moral flexibility yields power that is monstrous; in *Antony and Cleopatra* social theory that denies the value of irrationality is shown to be arid; in *King Lear* commodification proves hazardous, and the wisdom of pursing progress through change is questioned. Arguably, this question is answered in *The Tempest*, where "utopia" is revealed to be a variation on our current oppression. Shackled to a mountain of debt to purchase "skills for employability" in a higher education system that is beset by insecurity over the status of knowledge, students of the neoliberal utopia are obliged to imitate the log-hauler Caliban, rather than his erudite master. Arguably, the greatest task faced by educators today is not to discover "what works" for employability in the market society, but how we might retain the Aristotelean buffer to instrumentality without promoting elitism. While there is no easy answer to the question, 'What is education for?' we cut off hope of cultivating a society that aims for anything higher than the accumulation of wealth if we concede to the neoliberal view that education is simply about gaining skills and credentials for employment.

Notes

1 Benda, J. in Collini, S. (2006) *Absent Minds: Intellectuals in Britain*. Oxford: Oxford University Press. p. 281.
2 Ibid.
3 Hirst, P.H. (1973: 90) 'Liberal Education and the Nature of Knowledge' In: Peters, R.S. (ed.) *The Philosophy of Education*. Oxford: Oxford University Press. pp. 87–111.
4 Ibid: 89.
5 James, W. (1979: 22) 'The Will to Believe' In: James, W. (ed.) *The Will to Believe and Other Essays in Popular Philosophy*. Cambridge, MA: Harvard University Press. pp. 13–33.
6 Ibid.
7 Ibid: 14.

8 Ibid.
9 Fairfield, P. (2009) *Education after Dewey*. London: Continuum International Publishing Group. p. 106.
10 Hirst (1973: 101).
11 Seneca, L.A. (1969: 156) 'Letter LXXXVIII' In: Campbell, R. (trans. & intro.) *Letters from a Stoic*. London: Penguin Books Ltd. pp. 151–161.
12 Ibid.
13 Bristol, M.D. (1990) *Shakespeare's America, America's Shakespeare*. London: Routledge. p. 37.
14 Ibid: 37.
15 Bevington, D. (2008) *Shakespeare's Ideas: More Things in Heaven and Earth*. Chichester: Wiley-Blackwell. p. 203.
16 Adams, R.M. (1989) *Shakespeare: The Four Romances*. New York, NY: W.W. Norton & Company Inc. p. xii.
17 Kastan, D.S. (2014) *A Will to Believe: Shakespeare and Religion*. Oxford: Oxford University Press.
18 Kinney, A.F. (1992: 154) 'Teaching *The Tempest* as the Art of "If" ' In: Hunt, M. (ed.) *Approaches to Teaching Shakespeare's the Tempest and Other Late Romances*. New York: Modern Language Association of America. pp. 153–159.
19 Aristotle (1967) '*Politics*: Book VII' In: Burnet, J. (ed. & trans.) *Aristotle on Education: Extracts from the Ethics and Politics*. Cambridge: Cambridge University Press. p. 111.
20 Heath, M. (2008) 'Aristotle on Natural Slavery' *Phronesis, 53*, pp. 243–270.
21 Seneca (1969: 151).
22 Heath (2008: 243).
23 Ibid.
24 Ibid: 268.
25 Cefalu, P. (2004) *Revisionist Shakespeare: Transitional Ideologies in Texts and Contexts*. Basingstoke: Palgrave Macmillan. p. 48.
26 Elton, G.R. (1971) *England under the Tudors*. London: Methuen & Co. Ltd.
27 Shershow, S.C. (2003) 'Work and the Gift: Notes toward an Investigation' In: Woodbridge, L. (ed.) *Money and the Age of Shakespeare*. Basingstoke: Palgrave Machmillan. pp. 97–112.
28 Dawson, K. & Wall, P. (1971) *The Problem of Poverty*. Oxford: Oxford University Press.
29 Bevington (2008: 209).
30 Seneca (1969) 'Letter XLVII' In: Campbell, R. (trans. & intro.) *Letters from a Stoic*. London: Penguin Books Ltd. p. 91.
31 Heath (2008: 262).
32 Ryan, K. (2015) *Shakespeare's Universality: Here's Fine Revolution*. London: Bloomsbury Arden Shakespeare. p. 11. Italics in original.
33 Illich, I. (2015) *Deschooling Society*. London: Marion Boyars Publishing Ltd. p. 32.
34 Ibid.
35 Ibid.
36 Ibid.
37 Ibid: 106.
38 Burnet, J. (1967) *Aristotle on Education: Extracts from the Ethics and Politics*. Cambridge: Cambridge University Press. p. 10.
39 Ibid.
40 Marrou, H.I. (1964) *A History of Education in Antiquity*. Lamb, G. (trans.). New York, NY: A Mentor Book by the New American Library. p. 91.
41 Ibid: 83.
42 Burnet (1967: 140).

43 Protagoras in Marrou (1964: 82).
44 Marrou (1964: 114).
45 Aristotle (1967) '*Ethics*: Book X' In: Burnet, J. (ed. & trans.) *Aristotle on Education: Extracts from the Ethics and Politics*. Cambridge: Cambridge University Press. p. 94.
46 Ibid.
47 Ibid.
48 Marrou (1964: 146).
49 Ibid.
50 Ibid.
51 Aristotle (1967) '*Politics*: Book VIII' In: Burnet, J. (ed. & trans.) *Aristotle on Education: Extracts from the Ethics and Politics*. Cambridge: Cambridge University Press. pp. 107–108.
52 Aristotle (1967) '*Politics*: Book VIII' In: Burnet, J. (ed. & trans.) *Aristotle on Education: Extracts from the Ethics and Politics*. Cambridge: Cambridge University Press. pp. 108–109.
53 Aristotle (1967: 108).
54 Ibid.
55 Lupset, T. (1956: 85) 'An Exhortation to Young Men' In: Nugent, E.M. (ed.) *The Thought & Culture of the English Renaissance*. Cambridge: Cambridge University Press. pp. 81–88.
56 Dewey, J. (2011) *Democracy and Education*. www.simonandbrown.com, p. 34.
57 Ibid.
58 Ibid.
59 Ibid.
60 Ibid.
61 Ibid: 44.
62 Dewey, J. (1960) *The Quest for Certainty*. New York: Capricorn. p. 196.
63 Dewey (2011: 68).
64 Ibid: 49.
65 Ibid: 48.
66 Ibid.
67 Ibid.
68 Larochelle, M. & Bednarz, N. (1998: 3) 'Constructivism and Education: Beyond Epistemological Correctness' In: Larochelle, M., Bednarz, N. & Garrison, J. (eds.) *Constructivism and Education*. Cambridge: Cambridge University Press. pp. 3–20.
69 Conduct, M. (2013: 109) 'Some Cautionary Words about Constructivism' *Commonwealth Education Partnerships 2012/2013*, pp. 108–110. Available online at: http://www.cedol.org/wp-content/uploads/2013/09/Some-cautionary-words-Conduct.pdf [Accessed 1st April 2016].
70 Philips, D.C. (1995: 5) 'The Good, the Bad, and the Ugly: The Many Faces of Constructivism' *Educational Researcher, 24* (7), pp. 5–12.
71 Ibid: 9.
72 Ibid: 11.
73 Ibid.
74 Williams, J. (2016) *Academic Freedom in an Age of Conformity*. Basingstoke: Palgrave Macmillan.
75 Devitt, M. in Conduct (2013: 108).
76 Ibid: 59.
77 Kennedy in Williams (2016: 59).
78 DfEE & QCA (1999) *The National Curriculum: Handbook for Secondary Teachers in England*. London: Department for Education and Employment and Qualifications and Curriculum Authority.

79 Griffith, R. (2000) *National Curriculum – National Disaster?: Education and Citizenship.* London: RoutledgeFalmer. p. 13.

80 Ibid: 8.

81 Ibid.

82 Yeomans, D. (2002) *Constructing Vocational Education: From TVEI to GNVQ.* Leeds: University of Leeds Post 14 Research Group.

83 Ward, S.C. (2010) *Understanding Creative Partnerships: An Examination of Policy and Practice.* Doctoral Thesis, Durham University.

84 Major, J. (1991) Conservative Party Conference Speech 1991. Available online at: http://www.johnmajor.co.uk/speechconf1991.html [Accessed 18th August 2010].

85 Marquand, D. (2014) *Mammon's Kingdom: An Essay on Britain, Now.* London: Allen Lane. p. 106.

86 Hayek (2011).

87 Philips (1995: 5).

88 Hayek, F.A. (2011) *The Constitution of Liberty: The Definitive Edition.* Hamowy, R. (ed.). Chicago: The University of Chicago Press. p. 74.

89 Gove, M. (2013) 'The Progressive Betrayal' Speech to Social Market Foundation, 5th February 2013. Available online at: http://www.smf.co.uk/michael-gove-speaks-at-the-smf/ [Accessed 16th April 2016].

90 Ibid.

91 Ibid.

92 National Research Council (2012) *Education for Life and Work: Developing Transferable Knowledge and Skills in the 21st Century.* Committee on Defining Deeper Learning and 21st Century Skills, Pellegrino, J.W & Hilton, M.L. (eds.). Washington, DC: The National Academies Press. p. 74.

93 Bristol (1990: 38).

94 Sinfield, A. (2003: 164) 'Give an Account of Shakespeare and Education . . .' In: Dollimore, J. & Sinfield, A. (eds.) *Political Shakespeare: Essays in Cultural Materialism.* Manchester: Manchester University Press. pp. 158–181.

95 Law, S. (2006) *The War for Children's Minds.* Abingdon: Routledge. p. 124.

96 Ryan, K. in Law (2006: 126).

97 Collini, S. (2012) *What Are Universities For?* London: Penguin Books Ltd.

98 Dewey (2011: 34).

99 Heath (2008: 251) Italics in original.

100 Ibid.

101 Seneca (1969) 'Letter LXXXVIII' In: Campbell, R. (trans. & intro.) *Letters from a Stoic.* London: Penguin Books Ltd. p. 151.

102 Siedentop, L. (2015) *Inventing the Individual: The Origins of Western Liberalism.* London: Penguin, p. 42.

103 Berlin, I. (2007: 62) 'Political Ideas in the Twentieth Century' In: Hardy, H. (ed.) *Liberty: Isaiah Berlin.* Oxford: Oxford University Press. pp. 55–93.

104 Seneca (1969: 151).

105 Clinton, B. (1992) In: Kennedy, S. (2014) 'A Forgotten Lesson: It's the Economy, Stupid'. Available online at: http://inequality.org/economy-stupid/ [Accessed 28th April 2016].

106 Rand, A. (2007) *The Fountainhead.* London: Penguin Books Ltd. p. 492.

107 Ibid.

108 Ibid.

109 Ibid.

110 Piketty, T. (2014) *Capital in the Twenty-First Century.* Goldhammer, A. (trans.). London: The Belknap Press of Harvard University.

111 Habermas, J. (1981) 'Modernity versus Postmodernity' New German Critique, 22 Special Issue on Modernism, pp. 3–14. Translated by Seyla Ben-Habib.

112 Ibid: 7.
113 Ibid.
114 Ibid: 8.
115 Hayek, F.A. (2007) *The Road to Serfdom. Text and Documents: The Definitive Edition*. Chicago: The University of Chicago Press. p. 68.
116 Vaughan, V.M. & Vaughan, A.T. (1999) 'Introduction' In: Vaughan, V.M. & Vaughan, A.T. (eds.) *The Arden Shakespeare: The Tempest*. London: Thomson Learning. pp. 1–138.
117 Montaigne 'Of the Caniballes' In: Vaughan, V.M. & Vaughan, A.T. (eds.) (1999: 303–314).
118 Illich (2015: 103) See also *The Tempest* (5.1.183).

Conclusion

Through this book, I hope to have demonstrated that it is not necessary for us to *invent* a riposte to neoliberalism, as it already exists in Shakespeare's plays. According to Michael Bristol, 'Knowledge is a kind of transgression in so far as it departs from the received wisdom accumulated by a culture or community over time'.[1] I would argue that, today, Shakespeare is our most transgressive writer. Fundamentally conservative in outlook,[2] Shakespeare did not depart from the received wisdom of his day, which was largely informed by medieval sensibilities.[3] Instead, he critiqued the newly emergent ideology of capitalism[4] and considered the robustness of alternate value systems in the nascent market society.[5] Consequently, the knowledge imparted by Shakespeare is perhaps more transgressive *today* that it was when he wrote his plays, as they challenge our more fully fledged capitalist ideas about what it means to be an 'individual man *qua* man'.[6] The 400th anniversary celebrations of Shakespeare's death appear to confirm Ben Jonson's claim that Shakespeare 'was not of an age, but for all time',[7] yet it would be naïve to suppose that the popularity of Shakespeare's plays means that his ideas are likely to inform educational policy today, for a number of reasons. First, if we subscribe to Hayek's theory of social evolution, then we are likely to believe that we have progressed *beyond* the medieval theocentric worldview depicted in plays such as *Macbeth* and *King Lear*, and to hold Shakespeare in affection as part of our cultural heritage, rather than as someone who might speak to our present situation. Second, Shakespeare's depiction of divine and natural law is incompatible with our current embrace of constructivist theory about knowledge. Third, the postmodern theory of power relations has captivated educational researchers so that both praise and condemnation of the neoliberal project are based upon ideas that are antithetical to Shakespeare's depiction of unity as a buffer to instrumentality. In this conclusion I offer an analysis of these blocks to the transformation of education, and indicate avenues for future research that draw upon the themes explored in this book.

1. Hayek's theory of social evolution

In Chapter 1 it was noted that Hayek's rejection of the rationalist position entailed his alignment with anti-rational theory, which he describes as being 'closer to the Christian tradition of the fallibility and sinfulness of man'.[8] Hayek's aversion to

the rationalist tradition was not shared by other neoliberal economists and philosophers, and Buchanan's scepticism over 'transcendental common bliss'[9] and
Rand's aversion to what she saw as immoral Naturalism helped form what might
be described as the neoliberal consensus that the exercise of human reason is not
subject to supernatural governance. Both *Hamlet* and *Macbeth* are, of course,
famous for their supernatural spectacle, but the role that supernatural knowledge plays in these dramas is dissimilar to the anti-rational theory advocated by
Hayek, despite its Christian antecedents. For Hayek, the individual chooses to
follow rules that have yielded favourable results over time, not for their transcendental properties, but because it is beyond the capacity of human reason to
know what depends upon the observance of those rules. The neoliberal concept
of the heroic entrepreneur is thus predicated upon the belief that the individual
is an autonomous agent who is not *compelled* to action by the kind of mysticism
explored by Shakespeare, but instead capitalises upon his observation of other
people's behaviour to further his own interests. In the context of education, the
individual's heroic mission is to gain skills and credentials to become a "winner"
in the zero-sum game of employability.

According to Hayek, socialism's archaic discourse of interdependence threatens the future of Western civilization by failing to acknowledge that technological
progress is made possible through creative individuals' cooperation with *abstract*
rules of conduct, rather than adherence to concrete common aims.[10] Being
"modern" thus requires us to reject, like Machiavelli, the kind of 'tribal ethics'[11]
that are violated in *Macbeth* and instead adapt our instincts to new events. Machiavelli's ideas about leadership were an affront to the medieval theocentric worldview, but if we subscribe to Hayek's theory of social evolution, we might describe
Machiavellianism as a "social mutation" that has been reproduced to the point of
saturation because of its "fitness for purpose", so that present-day thought carries the gene of Machiavelli's radical thinking. In their analysis of the relationship
between crime and creativity, David H. Cropley and Arthur J. Cropley appear to
endorse Hayek's pragmatic outlook, conceptualised as 'the evolutionary view of
morals'.[12] According to Cropley and Cropley:

> . . . moral precepts are not physical laws or forces of nature such as gravity,
> but are ideals that have been worked out by philosophers, religious authori-
> ties, or other thinkers, and in this sense they reflect the influence of religion
> or philosophy, culture, family, and friends, are subjective, and liable to change
> over time or in different societies. They are a matter of subjective internal
> conviction rather than concrete evidence or physical or even legal coercion.[13]

This outlook complements Machiavelli's scepticism over divine and natural law,
which forms the basis of moral flexibility. Thus, in our current market society
we may enjoy Shakespeare's depiction of good and evil in plays such as *Macbeth* while feeling content that the insights of pragmatism have taken us beyond
this simple binary into a more highly evolved and complex engagement with
ethics. Policy on school leadership appears to endorse this evolutionary model

by defining contemporary social justice as a private matter that requires behavioural management, rather than a collective concern, and in the discourse of school leadership "success" is positioned as the outcome of the personal efficacy of school leaders in competition with one another. Hayek described himself as pragmatic, rather than unprincipled, and cautioned that the market society cannot function effectively without 'deeply engrained moral beliefs'.[14] New Public Management has attempted to ensure that the exercise of moral flexibility is not tyrannical, yet commentators have argued that it is not possible to simultaneously follow Judeo-Christian ethics and build a successful enterprise under neoliberalism, as moral flexibility is incompatible with obedience to religious edicts.[15] Irrespective of one's religious convictions, it is difficult to see how the cultivation of an "aggregate of competing individuals" will promote social justice.

King Lear seems to foreshadow Hayek's anti-rationalist theory by refusing to present either mysticism *or* human reason as reliable guides to action. The catastrophic events depicted in *King Lear* arguably illustrate the danger of wholeheartedly endorsing the Cropleys' theory of 'internal subjective conviction' and the belief that moral flexibility is an evolutionary enhancement to the human condition. By contrasting the Stoics' faith in universal natural law with Machiavellianism, Shakespeare seems to imply that the equilibrium of the market society is predicated upon the disavowal of the collective gift of nature's bounty and the acceptance of the theory of scarcity. The fear of having and being "nothing" may, perhaps, inspire the neoliberal entrepreneur to heroically embrace risk in the market society, but it more commonly provokes anxiety over the accruement of credentials in the zero-sum game of employability, and it is perhaps telling that *King Lear* has been described by critics as Shakespeare's most pessimistic play.[16] Nevertheless, the popularity of the evolutionary view of morals presents a seemingly insurmountable barrier to the development of non-Machiavellian education policy that is simultaneously held to be "modern".

2. Social constructivist theory

The classical model of liberal education rested on the belief that knowledge is the understanding of reality. Today it seems we are more likely to share the pragmatists' belief that our responsiveness to a hypothesis is dependent upon its relationship to our existing beliefs and proclivities, rather than its intrinsic properties. The "modern" idea that moral precepts are 'a matter of internal subjective conviction' is consistent with the theory of constructivism, which holds that knowledge is an organisation of concepts, expectations and abilities that enables successful coping with the world. In *The Social Construction of Reality*, published in 1966, Peter Berger and Thomas Luckman make the following assertion:

> I encounter knowledge in everyday life as socially distributed, that is, as possessed differently by different individuals and types of individuals. I do not share my knowledge equally with all my fellowmen, and there may be some knowledge that I share with no one.[17]

The belief that knowledge is possessed differently by different people has led to the emergence of identity politics around such things as gender, race and sexuality. According to identity politics, identity is not a 'fixed inner essence' but 'a series of masks, roles and potentialities, a kind of amalgam of everything which is provisional, contingent and improvisatory'.[18] Philosophers have described this perspective as 'postmodern',[19] and have largely welcomed the demise of overarching theories to explain the human condition, such as "natural and divine law". Not everyone, however, has been willing to concur with Lyotard that 'Consensus has become an outmoded and suspect value'[20] and embrace the more fashionable concept of difference. For example, Peter Barry contrasts the fluidity of identity politics with the arguably more coherent class-based politics centred on situations, such as low-pay;[21] Todd Gitlin laments the social atomisation that has resulted from the celebration of difference,[22] and even exponents of "voice", such as Nick Couldry, have expressed concern that not all voices are valued equally in the market society.[23] Notwithstanding such concerns, both constructivism and Hayek's instrumental account of knowledge as a means to optimise our expression of free choice in the market mechanism are manifest in education policy today. Under neoliberalism, knowledge is not the *goal* of education: instead, educators are encouraged to valorise students' subjective response to knowledge as a means of economic self-actualisation, or "employability", which is conceptualised as the end of education. The difficulty for educational researchers is how to counter the neoliberal argument that knowledge is socially distributed and underpins individuals' relative performance in the free market without expressing what might be described as old-fashioned and baseless ideas about knowledge. The idea that we might turn to literature such as Shakespeare's plays to challenge instrumental accounts of knowledge has, itself, been destabilised by postmodernism. In his treatise on literary theory, published in 1983, Terry Eagleton claims that 'Anything can be literature, and anything which is regarded as unalterably and unquestionably literature – Shakespeare for example – can cease to be literature'.[24]

3. Postmodern theory of power

In Chapter 2, Foucault's genealogy of power relations was considered in relation to *Measure for Measure* and performativity in schools. Victor Tadros contrasts Foucault's analysis of power with jurisprudential scholarship that has 'not accounted for the *historical differences* in law's evolution'[25] and praises Foucault's concept of discipline which, he says, 'both constructs the subject and subjects him to subtle forms of control'.[26] There is, it seems, a fit between Foucault's concept of power and constructivist accounts of identity that, together with Hayek's theory of social evolution, form a powerful rejoinder to what Tadros describes as 'an archaic vision of society'.[27] The discussion of power has become the defining feature of educational research today. Researchers who endorse the neoliberal project aim to identify "what works" in order to make the link between education and employability stronger, while neoliberalism's detractors condemn the erosion of teachers' autonomy and the impact of accountability measures on marginalised pupils. Foucault identifies the Renaissance as the point of transition from pastoral to modern modalities of power, and social evolution theory seems to imply that Shakespeare's Renaissance humanism is archaic, making it difficult to apply insights from *Measure for Measure* and *Antony and Cleopatra* when considering if educational researchers should, or should not, focus on power relations.

Two books published in the 400th anniversary year of Shakespeare's death – *The Power Paradox* by Dacher Keltner and *The Path* by Michael Puett and Christine Gross-Loh – arguably constitute a challenge to our current faith in social evolution, and in particular the development of ideas about power. In stark contrast to Rand, Keltner argues that altruism is the basis for gaining and maintaining power, and he rejects the "survival of the fittest" model of power handed down to us by Machiavelli:

> Whereas the Machiavellian approach to power assumes that individuals grab it through coercive force, strategic deception, and the undermining of others, the science finds that power is not grabbed but is given to individuals by groups.[28]

Keltner cites evidence from psychology studies to support his argument that true power lies in making a difference in the world and that the 'most direct path to enduring power is through generosity'.[29] Although this view is consistent with Keltner's rejection of Machiavelli's advice in *The Prince*, his claim that Machiavellianism cannot account for the rise of the civil rights, women's rights, and gay rights movements is debatable, as moral flexibility supports, rather than suppresses, the pursuit of self-interest. Arguably, the emergence of identity politics reflects the widespread endorsement of moral flexibility, rather than undermines Machiavellianism. Nevertheless, Keltner's critique of our beliefs about power in neoliberal societies indicates a shift in thinking about the purported ethical neutrality of the market mechanism. This shift is, perhaps, more pronounced in Puett and Gross-Loh's book. In their analysis of Laozi's theory of unity, known as The Way, Puett and Gross-Loh make a statement that could be a summary of the message conveyed by *Measure for Measure* and *Antony and Cleopatra*:

> Strength and domination render us incapable of relating to others and the things around us. The instant we see the world as a set of overt power balances, the instant we have differentiated ourselves from others – whether through imposing our will, competitiveness, or estrangement – we have lost the Way.[30]

Puett and Gross-Loh's analysis reveals the danger of adopting a Foucauldian theory of governance, in which we see the world in terms of overt power balances, as this outlook brings disequilibrium into being. It is better, they argue, for us to recognise our human connectivity than to articulate our differences. In *Measure for Measure* the scales of justice evoked by the play's title are balanced when the disguises and deceptions that empowered both the Duke and Angelo are shed and the characters connect person-to-person. In *Antony and*

Cleopatra, the failure of the characters to connect person-to-person results in a hollow victory for Octavius, who ends the play alone. To paraphrase Tacitus, Octavius made a wasteland and called it peace. Puett and Gross-Loh claim that Confucius, Socrates and the Buddha addressed similar philosophical questions in response to similar 'societal catalysts'[31] at roughly the same time, and we might therefore expect to find parallels between ancient Chinese ideas about power and Shakespeare's depiction of governance. The challenge for educational researchers is how to respond to Puett and Gross-Loh's theory that we may impact the world by "connecting with everything", and Keltner's model of distributed "compassionate" power, without attracting derision for appearing to endorse what Eagleton describes as Shakespeare's 'ridiculously sanguine ideology of Nature'.[32]

In a progressive society, says Hayek, 'some must lead, and the rest must follow',[33] yet the march of progress imagined by Hayek appears to be something of a regression, as following Machiavelli's lead takes us back to the instrumentality condemned by Plato and Aristotle in the fourth century BC. Our unease over the concept of the "natural slave" is perhaps a legitimate argument against liberal education as a buffer to instrumentality, and indeed Caliban's eloquent resentment of his servitude in *The Tempest* hints at the complexity of classical ideas about human relations in the cosmic "chain of being". Nowadays most people share Dewey's contempt for education that positions elite children as "worthy" of theoretical contemplation and ordinary children as their future servants. However, Shakespeare's comic handling of the concept of utopia in *The Tempest* serves to remind us that attempts to improve our situation often result in a replication of current forms of oppression. Arguably, neoliberalism's narrow focus on employability, which is underpinned by constructivist theory, risks ensuring that *all* students receive an education to equip them for a life of servitude, which is hardly the utopia envisioned by followers of Dewey. The challenge for educational researchers is to discover a means to reanimate debate about the purpose of education without appearing to endorse offensive ideas about social privilege, so that the discourse of education once again includes the cultivation of more than just employability. Through this book I hope to have demonstrated both the enormity of this task and the possibility of drawing inspiration from Shakespeare when considering alternatives to neoliberal ideology. Today, of course, we cannot *make* ourselves trust in the abundant universe or believe in the "magic womb" of liberal education; we cannot *force* ourselves to feel awe in response to divine and natural law or place our faith in gift-exchange. All of these possibilities were alive to Shakespeare's contemporaries and form part of the rich contexture of the plays explored in this book. We can, however, recognise that the blanket acceptance of Hayek's theory of social evolution risks undermining attempts to find an alternative to Machiavellian pragmatism.

Notes

1 Bristol, M.D. (1990) *Shakespeare's America, America's Shakespeare*. London: Routledge. p. 39.
2 Hawkes, D. (2015) *Shakespeare and Economic Theory*. London: Bloomsbury Publishing Plc. p. 123.

3 Hooker, R. in Dollimore, J. (2003: 81) 'Transgression and Surveillance in *Measure for Measure*' In: Dollimore, J. & Sinfield, A. (eds.) *Political Shakespeare: Essays in Cultural Materialism*. Second Edition. Manchester: Manchester University Press. pp. 72–87.

4 Hawkes (2015).

5 Engle, L. (1993) *Shakespearean Pragmatism: Market of His Time*. Chicago: The University of Chicago Press.

6 Hayek, F.A. (2007) *The Road to Serfdom. Text and Documents: The Definitive Edition*. Chicago: The University of Chicago Press. p. 68.

7 Jonson, B. in Baldwin, T.W. (1944) *William Shakspere's Small Latine & Lesse Greeke*. Urbana: University of Illinois Press. p. 2.

8 Hayek, F.A. (2011) *The Constitution of Liberty: The Definitive Edition*. Hamowy, R. (ed.). Chicago: The University of Chicago Press. p. 120.

9 Buchanan, J.M. (2000) *The Limits of Liberty: Between Anarchy and Leviathan*. Indianapolis: Liberty Fund Inc. p. 3.

10 Gamble, A. (1996) *Hayek: The Iron Cage of Liberty*. Cambridge: Polity Press.

11 Ibid: 45.

12 Cropley, D.H. & Cropley, A.J. (2013) *Creativity and Crime: A Psychological Analysis*. Cambridge: Cambridge University Press. p. 132.

13 Ibid.

14 Hayek (2011: 123).

15 Galie, P.J. & Bopst, C. (2006) 'Machiavelli & Modern Business: Realist Thought in Contemporary Corporate Leadership Manuals' *Journal of Business Ethics*, 65, pp. 235–250.

16 Bradley, A.C. (1987) 'From *Shakespearean Tragedy*' In: Fraser, R. (ed.) *William Shakespeare: The Tragedy of King Lear*. New York, NY: Signet Classic. pp. 225–242.

17 Berger, P.L. & Luckman, T. (1984) *The Social Construction of Reality: A Treatise in the Sociology of Knowledge*. London: Penguin Books Ltd. p. 60.

18 Barry, P. (2009) *Beginning Theory: An Introduction to Literary and Cultural Theory*. Third Edition. Manchester: Manchester University Press. p. 140.

19 Lyotard, J.F. (2005) *The Postmodern Condition: A Report on Knowledge*. Bennington, G. & Massumi, B. (trans.). Manchester: Manchester University Press.

20 Ibid: 66.

21 Barry (2009).

22 Gitlin, T. (1995) *The Twilight of Common Dreams: Why America is Wracked by Culture Wars*. New York: Metropolitan Books.

23 Couldry, N. (2010) *Why Voice Matters: Culture and Politics after Neoliberalism*. London: SAGE Publications Ltd.

24 Eagleton, T. (2008) *Literary Theory: An Introduction*. Anniversary Edition. Minneapolis: University of Minnesota Press. p. 9.

25 Tadros, V. (1998: 77) 'Between Governance and Discipline: The Law and Michel Foucault' *Oxford Journal of Legal Studies*, 18 (1), pp. 75–103. Italics in original.

26 Ibid: 78.

27 Ibid.

28 Keltner, D. (2016) *The Power Paradox: How We Gain and Lose Influence*. London: Allen Lane. p. 43.

29 Ibid: 167.

30 Puett, M. & Gross-Loh, C. (2016) *The Path: A New Way to Think About Everything*. London: Penguin Random House UK. p. 103.

31 Ibid: 16.

32 Eagleton, T. (1986) *William Shakespeare*. Oxford: Basil Blackwell Ltd. p. 99.

33 Hayek (2011: 98).

Plot summaries

1. Hamlet

Guards tell Horatio that they have seen a ghost upon the battlements of Elsinore castle that resembles the father of Hamlet, Prince of Denmark. Mourning his father and dismayed by his mother Gertrude's sudden marriage to his uncle Claudius, who is now King of Denmark, Hamlet hastens to the battlements to speak with his dead father. The ghost tells Hamlet he was murdered by his brother Claudius and demands revenge. Swearing his friend Horatio to secrecy, Hamlet vows to kill his uncle and feign madness to cover this deed.

News reaches Elsinore of a claim made by Fortinbras of Norway upon the lands won from his father by the late king. Claudius dispatches envoys to Norway, and Gertrude dissuades Hamlet from returning to university. Laertes, son of Claudius' counsellor Polonius, leaves for France. Bidding farewell to his sister Ophelia, Laertes cautions her against taking her romance with Hamlet too seriously or too far. Believing that love may be the cause of Hamlet's troubled mind, Polonius advises Claudius and Gertrude to stage an encounter between the lovers and covertly observe events. This encounter is brutal: affecting madness, Hamlet speaks cruelly to Ophelia, thereby disproving Polonius' conjecture that love is the source of his malady.

Hoping that convivial company might lift Hamlet's spirits, and seeking to uncover the cause of his bleak mood, Claudius and Gertrude invite two of his university friends, Guildenstern and Rosencrantz, to Elsinore. Guessing that these friends have been sent to spy on him, Hamlet deals harshly with them. Hamlet is heartened by the arrival of the travelling players: struggling to determine the veracity of the ghost's claims, Hamlet asks one of the actors to insert a scene into their performance to test his uncle's guilt. This scene closely resembles the murder of Hamlet's father, and yields the proof that Hamlet seeks when Claudio curtails the performance. Distressed by the evening's events, Gertrude summons Hamlet to her room. On his way, Hamlet observes Claudius alone at prayer, but he lets slip this chance to kill his uncle, fearing that death at prayer might send his soul to heaven. Instead, he makes his way to his mother's room, where he upbraids Gertrude for her choice of second husband. Thinking that Claudius is eavesdropping, Hamlet stabs his sword through a curtain and discovers that he has instead killed Polonius. The ghost of Hamlet's father chastises Hamlet for his failure to exact revenge.

Claudius sends Hamlet to England with Rosencrantz and Guildenstern. Discovering his death warrant on the ship, Hamlet substitutes his friends' names for his own. During his absence, Ophelia becomes mad with grief over the loss of her father and drowns herself. Having escaped from the ship, Hamlet meets up with Horatio at the graveyard where Ophelia is brought for burial. Laertes, who has returned from France, is enraged by the sight of Hamlet protesting love for his sister at her grave. A duel is arranged, and Claudius persuades Laertes to employ a poisoned rapier to guarantee Hamlet's death. To make doubly sure of success, Claudius poisons a goblet of wine to be offered to Hamlet, which is unwittingly drunk by Gertrude. Hamlet is struck by the poisoned rapier, but in the confusion of the fight the swords are exchanged and Laertes is likewise struck. Seeing the collapse of Gertrude, Laertes discloses foul play, and Hamlet stabs Claudius and forces him to drink the remaining poison. Dying, Hamlet asks Horatio to tell the world his story. Fortinbras arrives and is astounded to discover that his noble adversaries are dead.

2. Measure for Measure

In Vienna, the law against fornication is being ignored. Troubled by the licentiousness of his people but not wishing to lose their love, Duke Vincentio of Vienna feigns the need for overseas travel and appoints his punctilious deputy, Angelo, to rule in his absence. Angelo duly proclaims his intention to revive the law against fornication, and sentences Claudio to death for impregnating his fiancée, Juliet. Claudio's sister, the novice Isabella, learns of his predicament and leaves the nunnery to plead with Angelo for mercy. Consumed by lust for Isabella, Angelo tells her that he will pardon Claudio on condition that she surrenders her virginity to him. Isabella refuses, and hurries to the prison to tell Claudio to prepare for his death. Unbeknownst to Isabella, the Duke has disguised himself as a friar to observe the effect of Angelo's rule, and overhears her account of Angelo's proposal. The disguised Duke advises Isabella to accept Angelo's offer, and says that he will arrange for Angelo's forsaken fiancée, Marianna, to impersonate Isabella and sleep with Angelo under the cover of darkness. This substitution, he says, is not sinful, as Marianna was contracted to be Angelo's wife.

Meanwhile, Angelo orders the closure of Vienna's brothels and forces the notorious pimp, Pompey, to abandon his bawdy trade and serve the state as executioner. Angelo decides to break his promise to Isabella, and demands that the head of Claudio is brought to him after his romantic tryst. The disguised Duke intervenes, persuading the prison governor to execute the condemned drunkard Barnadine and deliver his head to Angelo instead. The disguised Duke visits Barnadine to prepare him to meet God, but is dismissed out of hand. Discovering that another prisoner has died of natural causes, *his* head is sent to Angelo. The disguised Duke tells Isabella that Angelo has deceived her, and that Claudio is dead. Distraught, Isabella and Marianna decide to inform the Duke of Angelo's wickedness. The Duke, now in his proper garments, makes a pretence of arriving in Vienna. Hearing Marianna and Isabella's tale, the Duke says he will have Angelo executed to balance the loss of Claudio. The ladies beg for mercy, whereupon the Duke reveals that Claudio is in fact still alive. The Duke commands Angelo to marry Marianna, and proposes marriage to Isabella.

3. Macbeth

King Duncan's generals, Macbeth and Banquo, encounter three witches upon a moor who predict that Macbeth will become Thane of Cawdor and King of Scotland, and that Banquo's descendants will one day rule Scotland. The first prophesy is immediately fulfilled when messengers reveal that Macbeth has been named Thane of Cawdor by Duncan in thanks for his courage in battle. Macbeth writes to his wife, Lady Macbeth, to inform her of this strange turn of events, and she is thrilled by the prospect of power. King Duncan comes to stay in Macbeth's castle, and Lady Macbeth urges her husband to seize this opportunity to fulfil the witches' prophesy by killing Duncan in his sleep. Against his better judgment, Macbeth stabs Duncan and points the finger of blame at Duncan's sons, Malcolm and Donalbain, who flee to England and Ireland.

Macbeth is crowned King of Scotland. Troubled by the witches' prediction that Banquo's heirs will rule Scotland, Macbeth has Banquo killed in an ambush but his son Fleance escapes. At dinner, Macbeth sees the ghost of Banquo and quits his place at the table. Increasingly fearful of losing his grip on power and subject to awful visions, Macbeth decides to visit the witches to learn more about his fate. Macbeth is pleased when the witches tell him that he cannot be killed by any man born of woman and is safe until Birnam wood comes to Dunsinane hill. Macbeth becomes increasingly tyrannical, ordering the murder of the family of Macduff, who has fled to England to join Malcom in raising an army against Macbeth. Meanwhile, Lady Macbeth has become a sleepwalker, perpetually washing phantom blood from her hands, and commits suicide. Macbeth is dismayed to see Malcom's army advancing upon Dunsinane hill shielded by branches of Birnam wood, thereby fulfilling the witches' prophesy. Buoyed by the knowledge that he cannot be killed by any man born of woman, Macbeth fights with confidence until Macduff reveals that he was ripped from his mother's womb. The pair duel and Macduff is victorious: Macbeth's head is presented to Malcolm, who is crowned king.

4. Antony and Cleopatra

Following victory in battle, Mark Antony has become one of the three rulers, or triumvirs, of the Roman Empire, along with Octavius Caesar and Lepidus. Antony is ruler of the eastern third of the empire and has fallen in love with the glamorous Queen of Egypt, Cleopatra, with whom he lives in Alexandria. On hearing of the death of his wife Fulvia and a rebellion led by Pompey, Antony returns to Rome. To prove his allegiance to Octavius, Antony marries Octavius' sister, Octavia. This marriage enrages Cleopatra, but on hearing that Octavia is cold, Cleopatra is confident that she will win back her lover.

The triumvirs meet with Pompey to negotiate peace in a drunken revelry on board Pompey's boat. Pompey's associate, Menas, suggests that they take advantage of this opportunity to murder the triumvirs, but Pompey refuses to act so dishonourably. Antony and Octavia depart for Athens, whereupon Octavius reneges on his word and declares war on Pompey, whom he defeats. Antony is furious when he discovers that Octavius used Lepidus to fight against Pompey, and then accused Lepidus of treason and seized his portion of the empire. Octavia implores Antony to maintain peace with her brother, but Antony sends her to Rome and re-joins his lover in Egypt. Enraged by this insult to his sister, Octavius declares war on Antony and Cleopatra. Cleopatra's navy is no match for Octavius' fleet, and Antony turns around his boat when he sees Cleopatra's ships sailing away from the battle. Antony is defeated. Believing that Cleopatra has betrayed him, Antony vows to kill her. Cleopatra flees to her mausoleum and sends a message to Antony saying that she is dead. Heartbroken, Antony commands his servant Eros to kill him, but Eros falls on his sword instead. Antony attempts suicide but is unsuccessful. Grievously wounded, Antony is carried by his followers to Cleopatra's mausoleum, where he dies in her arms. Resolving that she will not be captured by Octavius and paraded through Rome as his exotic trophy, Cleopatra forces a venomous snake to bite her. Octavius arrives and finds the dead lovers. Overawed by the loss of such a remarkable man and woman, Octavius orders them to be buried together with all due ceremony.

5. King Lear

Lear, the elderly King of Britain, decides to abdicate in favour of his three daughters, Goneril, Regan and Cordelia, and asks his daughters to say how much they love him so that he may distribute his kingdom accordingly. Goneril and Regan make extravagant protestations of their love and are duly awarded with land. Lear's youngest child, Cordelia, declares that she loves her father as much as a daughter should, and no more. Enraged by Cordelia's paltry tribute, Lear disowns Cordelia and divides her portion of Britain between her sisters. The Duke of Kent condemns Lear's action, and is banished. Now dowerless, Cordelia is rejected by her suitor, the Duke of Burgundy. Her other suitor, the King of France, respects Cordelia's integrity and says that he will marry her. Lear announces his intention to live alternately with Goneril, Duchess of Albany, and Regan, Duchess of Cornwall, attended by his retinue of one hundred knights, and commences his sojourn with Goneril.

Meanwhile, the Earl of Gloucester's illegitimate son, Edmund, is resentful of the fact that his legitimate brother, Edgar, will inherit their father's estate and so plans to discredit his brother. Edmund tells his father than Edgar is planning patricide. Unsettled by Lear's abdication and recent eclipses of the sun and moon, Gloucester believes Edmund. Edgar flees for his life disguised as a ragged madman.

Kent, disguised as a servant, returns and offers to serve Lear. Annoyed by the boisterous behaviour of Lear's retinue, Goneril asks her father to halve his number of followers. Incensed by Goneril's ingratitude, Lear declares that he will henceforth live with Regan and sets off for Gloucester's castle, where Regan and her husband Cornwall are guests. Goneril writes to inform her sister of their father's intemperance, and Edmund acts as a go-between for Goneril and Regan, who vie for his affection. Lear arrives and demands greater hospitality from Regan. Regan refuses to accommodate Lear with any followers whatsoever, and turns Lear and his Fool out of doors into a fierce storm. Gloucester pleads on Lear's behalf, and secretly instructs Kent to take Lear and the Fool to Dover where Cordelia has landed with a French army to rescue her father. Edmund persuades Cornwall and Regan that Gloucester is a traitor. Not daring to kill their host, instead they blind Gloucester and turn him out of doors. Wounded by a servant who came to Gloucester's aid, Cornwall dies.

Wandering the heath in the storm, Lear loses his mind. Lear, the Fool and Kent seek shelter in a hovel where they discover Edgar disguised as a mad beggar. The Fool tells Lear to go back to the castle and ask Regan for forgiveness, but he refuses, finding consolation in fanciful discourse with Edgar. Edgar discovers his blinded father upon the heath and offers to guide him to the coast. Gloucester asks to be taken to a cliff edge and imagines that he has plummeted to the beach below. Through this trick, Edgar persuades his father to value life over death. Gloucester and Edgar are joined by Lear, fantastically clad with wildflowers, and with Kent's aid Lear is reunited with Cordelia. Edgar reveals his true identity to his father, who dies, overcome with love and regret.

The French army is defeated. Lear and Cordelia are captured and sent to gaol by Edmund, but Lear expresses joy rather than regret over the prospect of captivity with Cordelia. Secretly, Goneril has written to Edmund asking him to kill Albany and marry her. To make sure that Edmund does not marry her sister instead, Goneril poisons Regan. Edgar, disguised as a knight, challenges Edmund to a duel and inflicts a mortal wound, whereupon Goneril commits suicide. With his dying breath, Edmund attempts to save Lear and Cordelia from the sentence he has imposed, but is too late. Cordelia has been hanged. Lear carries her body from the gaol, and looks in vain for a sign that Cordelia still lives. Heartbroken, Lear dies. Kent vows to follow his master. Albany and Edgar face the solemn task of rebuilding the kingdom.

6. The Tempest

A fierce storm at sea threatens to wreck a ship carrying a royal party bound for Italy headed by Alonso, King of Naples. Observing this calamity from a nearby island, Miranda implores her father, Prospero, to tell her why he has used his magic to raise the tempest. Prospero explains that he was once the Duke of Milan, but was overthrown by his brother, Antonio, to whom he had given the task of administering the state while he focused on his studies. Antonio conspired with Alonso, King of Naples, to kidnap Prospero and his motherless infant, Miranda, and cast them adrift at sea. The pair was saved by the kind old councillor, Gonzalo, who supplied them with food, clothing and Prospero's books of magic. Washed up upon the island, Prospero and Miranda have dwelled there a dozen years in the company of the monstrous Caliban, offspring of the dead witch Sycorax. Now, Prospero says, Fortune has brought his enemies within reach of his retribution.

Prospero charms Miranda to sleep and summons an airy spirit, Ariel, who tells Prospero that the people aboard the storm-tossed ship are alive and have been magically dispersed in diverse groups across the island. Ariel reminds Prospero of his vow to liberate him. Annoyed by this reminder, Prospero asks if he has forgotten that it was Prospero who freed him from the tree in which he had been cruelly imprisoned by Sycorax. Chastened, Ariel assumes the shape of a sea nymph visible only to his master, Prospero, and sets about his next commission. Woken from her sleep by Prospero, Miranda reluctantly consents to visit Caliban, her erstwhile pupil turned would-be sexual assailant. Prospero chides Caliban for his rude ways and forces him to fetch firewood. Ariel plays music that leads Ferdinand, son of the King of Naples, to Miranda. They instantly fall in love with one another, which pleases Prospero, but to ensure their spark of love is kindled into an enduring flame he contrives an impediment. Purporting to believe that Ferdinand is an imposter, Prospero tasks him with gathering firewood like the rough Caliban, much to Miranda's dismay.

Meanwhile, on another part of the island Alonso, his brother Sebastian, Antonio, Gonzalo and assorted courtiers are desperately searching for Ferdinand. Ariel plays music that sends everyone to sleep except Sebastian and Antonio. Antonio, Prospero's treacherous brother, points out to Sebastian that since Ferdinand is probably dead, Sebastian will become King of Naples if he kills Alonso. They draw their swords, but the sleepers are woken by Ariel and the party resumes its search for Ferdinand.

Elsewhere, Caliban encounters the jester Trinculo and the drunken servant Stephano. Caliban is given alcohol by Stephano, and all three become intoxicated. Caliban suggests that they kill Prospero, seize Miranda and claim the island as Stephano's kingdom. Ariel plays enticing music which they follow, leading them through bog and bramble. Alonso and his party, meanwhile, are exhausted by their search and are delighted to see a banquet conjured, unbeknownst to them, by Prospero. The tempting dishes vanish before they can be eaten, and Ariel, disguised as a harpy, chastises Antonio and Alonso for overthrowing Prospero.

Prospero releases Ferdinand from his log hauling duty, and consents to his marriage to Miranda. To celebrate their betrothal, Prospero conjures a masque. Suddenly recalling Caliban's plot to kill him, Prospero curtails the performance and commands Ariel to display a line of his fine clothes to trap his prospective assassins. When Stephano and Trinculo attempt to steal these clothes, they are, together with Caliban, chased off by a pack of spectral hounds set on by Prospero and Ariel. Prospero instructs Ariel to gather together the crew and passengers of the ship. Prospero rebukes Alonso, Antonio and Sebastian for their treachery, but says that he forgives them. Alonso laments the loss of his son Ferdinand, and is delighted when Prospero reveals Ferdinand and Miranda playing chess behind a curtain. The couple announce their engagement. Prospero releases Caliban, Stephano and Trinculo from Ariel's guard and forgives them too. The party agrees to sail for Italy the next day, with Prospero reinstated as the Duke of Milan. Prospero liberates Ariel, and bids the audience to likewise set him free through their applause.

Index

Adams, Robert 85
Adorno, Theodor 21, 53
alienation 21, 95
altruism 7, 35, 37, 40, 48, 105
anarchy: anarchism 2–3, 7, 16–17,
    19–20, 36, 49, 77
Ancient Greece 36, 66, 88, 89
anti-capitalist 21, 30, 35
anti-rationalist theory 17, 48, 51, 103
Apollonian 8, 66, 67
Apple, Michael 22, 30, 77
Aristotelean 89, 96
Aristotle 9, 52, 85, 86, 87, 88–9, 90,
    92, 93, 94, 106
Arnold, Matthew 36, 89, 91, 96
Athens 36, 112

Bacon, Francis 53, 54
Ball, Stephen 1, 7, 30, 75, 76, 78
Bardolatry 5
Barry, Peter 104
Bataille, George 74, 80
Becon, Thomas 70
Benda, Julien 84
Berger, Peter 103
Berlin, Isaiah 8, 58, 62, 64, 67
Bevington, David 4, 87
Blair, UK Prime Minister Tony 23, 24,
    63, 77
Bloom, Harold 5, 15, 19
Boas, Taylor 3
Bopst, Christopher 48
Bourdieu, Pierre 37
Bradley, A.C. 73
Brecht, Bertolt 5
Bristol, Michael i, 5, 84, 93, 101
Brown, Philip 24, 25
Buchanan, James M. 3, 7, 8, 16–17,
    20–1, 58, 62, 102
Buckley, William F. 21

Buddha 106
Burnet, John 88
Burns, Jennifer 22
Burrow, Colin 69
Bush, President George W. 32
Byron 62

Cable, Secretary of State for Business,
    Innovation and Skills Vince 60–2
Callaghan, Dympna 5
Callaghan, Prime Minister James 38
Camus, Albert 63
capitalism: capitalist i, 1, 4–6, 19, 21–3,
    35, 37, 66, 74, 80, 95, 101
Cefalu, Paul 86
chaos 17, 59, 74, 77
charisma: charismatic 7, 18–20, 22–3,
    25–6
Chomsky, Noam 1
chrematistics 70
Clinton, President Bill 94
coalition 59–62, 65–7
Cohen, Walter 60, 65
Coleridge, Samuel 20, 32, 36
Collini, Stephan 84
commensurability 71
commodification: commodify 1, 9, 60,
    61, 63, 69–80, 96
Conduct, Matthew 90
Confucius 106
connectivity 8, 35, 40, 52, 58, 62, 64,
    67, 72, 105
Conservative Party 13
constructivism: constructivist theory 9,
    90–2, 101, 103–4, 106
Couldry, Nick 104
countercultural 4, 21, 26, 37, 95
credentials for employment 7, 9, 23–4,
    64, 75, 76, 78, 79, 92, 94, 96, 102,
    103

Cropley, Arthur 102, 103
Cropley, David 102, 103
cultural materialism 4–5
culture 5, 18, 21, 36–7, 88–90, 93, 95,
    101, 102
culture wars 4, 5

Dale, Roger 37
Darwin, Charles: Darwinian 17, 35
Debord, Guy 21
DeGroot, Gerard 21, 22
Deleuze, Giles 77
Democrat 93
Denham, Andrew 13
deschooling 9, 37, 87, 95
Devitt, Michael 91
Dewey, John ix, 1, 9, 22, 35, 37–8, 40,
    84, 89–90, 94, 106
Dionysian 8, 66, 67
Dollimore, Jonathan 4, 31
Duby, Georges 46
duty 17–18, 35–6

economy i, 3, 22, 24–5, 63, 69, 76,
    93, 94
Education Endowment Foundation 77
Education Reform Act 33, 91
Education Schools Act 33
Elizabethan 4, 6
Elizabethan Poor Law 87
Ellis, Terry 37
eloquence 3–4
employability 24, 61, 64–5, 75, 76, 79,
    93, 94, 96, 102, 103, 104, 106
employment 23, 24, 84, 86, 87, 91, 92
Engle, Lars 69, 77
English, Fenwick 51
Enlightenment 3, 14, 21, 53, 61
enterprise education 22
entrepreneur: entrepreneurial 7, 9,
    13–14, 18–20, 22–5, 34, 44, 76, 78,
    80, 94, 96, 102, 103
equilibrium 8, 9, 40, 58, 74–5, 103;
    disequilibrium 105
equity 8, 25, 37, 53–4, 75
equivalence 70–1, 73, 74
Erasmus, Desiderius 4
Erkenntnis 36
Erlebnis 36
ethics 48, 52, 93, 102–3
Eudaimonia 86, 90
European Policy Network on School
    Leadership (EPNoSL) i

exchange-value 5, 69–72, 74, 80
executive: executive power 44, 45,
    49–51, 54

Fairfield, Paul 38
fascism 3, 36
Fenwick, Tara 33–4, 40
First Folio 4
Foakes, Reginald 45
Ford, Timothy 34
fortune 45–7, 72, 114
Foucauldian 105
Foucault, Michel 7, 31–3, 40, 104, 105
free choice 2–3, 8, 17, 21, 26, 34, 58,
    74, 104
freedom 3, 17, 18, 21, 22, 32–7, 39,
    44, 48, 51, 60, 62, 67, 74, 78, 94
Friedman, Milton 1, 3, 6–7, 22, 38,
    53, 95
friendship 52, 59
Froebel, Friedrich 35

Gaia 88
Galie, Peter 48
Galt, John 16
Gamble, Andrew 48, 49
Gans-Morse, Jordan 3
Gardner, Helen 5
Garnett, Mark 13
GCSEs 24
Gefühl 36
gift-exchange 9, 74
Gitlin, Todd 4, 104
god 19, 45–6, 53, 70, 110; demi-god
    40; goddess 3; godless 73, 80; gods
    77, 88, 90
Gove, Secretary of State for Education
    Michael 92
governance 1, 2, 7–8, 31–3, 40, 69, 95,
    102, 105–6
Gray, Hanna 3
Great Debate 38
Great Society 17, 48, 49
Greenblatt, Stephen 4, 13
Griffith, Rhys 91
Gross-Loh, Christine 105–6
Grubb, W. Norton 23
Guattari, Félix 77
Gyges 64

Habermas, Jürgen 94–5
Hall, Stuart 6
Hargreaves, David 77

Harvard Business School 13, 22
Harvard University 23, 91
Harvey, David 22, 78
Hawkes, David 69, 70
Heath, Malcolm 86
Hellenise 36
Hellenistic 88, 89
Her Majesty's Inspectorate (HMI) 33
heroic entrepreneur 7, 25, 44, 94, 102
Higher Education Funding Council for
    England (HEFCE) 60
High-stakes teacher evaluation (HSTE)
    32, 34
hippies: hippy movement 20–2, 37
Hirsch, E.D. 40
Hitler, Adolf 36
Hitler Youth 36
Holbrook, Peter 15, 32, 34
Holderness, Graham 6
Hooker, Richard 32
Horkheimer, Max 21, 53
House of Commons Select Committee
    24, 60
Hudson, Alan 60

identity politics 4–6, 91, 104–5
Illich, Ivan 9, 37, 87–8, 90, 95–6
individualism 4, 36, 40, 44, 49, 54, 64
Institute of Education Sciences (IES) 77
instrumentality 4, 45, 48, 80, 92, 94,
    96, 101, 106
International Monetary Fund (IMF) 24
investor-state dispute resolution
    (ISDS) 50
Isocrates 36

Jacobean 4, 6, 73
James, William 9, 84
Jay, Antony 8, 44, 54
Jeffrey, Bob 33, 34
Jones, Lord Digby 24
Jonson, Ben 4, 101
Joseph, Sir Keith 13, 20
Judeo-Christian ethics 48, 103
Jus natural 72

Kao, John 13, 22
Karpov, A.O. 75–6
Kastan, David Scott 85
Keltner, Dacher 105–6
Kennedy, President John F. 91
Keynesian economics 7
King James I 46

King's New School 4
Kinney, Arthur 85
Knights, L.C. 47, 52
knowledge 2, 8, 9, 15–16, 17, 24, 30,
    35–9, 48, 53, 54, 69, 74, 76, 84–96,
    101–4
Koopman, Colin 73, 77

laissez-faire capitalism 3, 17, 22, 26, 95
Laozi 105
Laski, Harold 36–7
law 2, 23, 31–2, 39, 40, 44–8, 53–4,
    104, 110
law, natural and divine 8, 9, 46–54,
    72–3, 101–4, 106
Law, Stephen 93
Lazerson, Marvin 23
leadership i, 8, 44–6, 50–1, 53–4, 93,
    102–3
Levin, Bernard 20
Levin, Richard 4
liberal education 4, 9, 84, 89–90, 93–4,
    103, 106
libertarian 19, 39
liberty ix, 2–3, 16, 17, 21, 34, 39, 58,
    62, 64, 71, 76, 92
Loomba, Ania 5
love, commodification of 9, 69–72
love, romantic 59, 66, 109–12, 114
love of learning 84–5
love of liberty 2, 32
Luckman, Thomas 103
Lupset, Thomas 88–9
Lyotard, Jean-François 65, 76–7, 78,
    80, 104

Machiavelli, Niccolò: Machiavellianism
    8, 9, 15, 20, 31, 44–54, 71, 73, 75,
    77, 80, 85, 93, 95, 102–3, 105–6
magic 13, 48, 85, 89, 113–14
'magic womb' 87–8, 90, 106
Major, Prime Minister John 33, 92
Mandelson, UK Trade and Industry
    Secretary Peter 23, 25
'man *qua* man' 44–5, 52, 95, 101
Mansfield, Harvey C. 45, 52
Marcus Aurelius Antonius ix, 53, 71–3
market-exchange 9, 74
marketisation 5–6, 8, 16, 58, 60, 62–5,
    72, 76
market mechanism i, 2, 3, 8, 17, 49–50,
    52–3, 58, 69, 71, 74–5, 77, 79–80,
    92, 96, 104–5

market order i, 1–2, 7
Market-Romantic 14, 16
Marrou, H.I. 88–9
Marx, Karl 4
meliorism 73, 76–7
Menon, Mahadi 5
meritocracy 23
Middle Ages 54
Montaigne, Michel de 15, 52, 95
Mont Pelerin Society 16
Montrose, Louis 6
moral flexibility 1, 8, 46–7, 50, 71, 96, 102–3, 105
moral law 45–6
More, Thomas 4
mysticism 14–15, 72, 102–3

National Curriculum 33, 91–2
National Research Council 93
National Socialists 36
naturalism 15, 102
natural selection 17, 49
natural slave 86–7, 89, 91, 106
nature 9, 45–7, 49, 52–4, 65–7, 69–70, 75, 84, 86, 94, 102–3, 106
Nazi: Nazism 36, 39, 44
negative liberty 8, 58, 62, 64
neoliberal education i, 1, 6–7, 25, 34, 91
neoliberalism i, 1–3, 6–9, 20, 22–4, 26, 33, 39, 44, 48, 53–4, 62, 78–80, 94–5, 101, 103–4, 106
New Economic Criticism 5–6
New Labour 24
New Public Management (NPM) 8, 49–50, 103
New Right 3
New Sociology of Education 37
Nietzsche, Friedrich 8, 66
Noakes, J. 36
No Child Left Behind 32–3
nothing: nothingness 9, 70, 72–5, 79–80, 103
Nozick, Robert 19, 23, 25
Nussbaum, Martha 59, 64, 66

Obama, President Barack 33
objectivist 16
Office for Standards in Education (OFSTED) 33
Olmedo, Antonio 30
Organisation for Economic Co-operation and Development (OECD) 24–5

Ortega y Gasset, J. 74
O'Toole, Fintan 64

Parks, Tim 45
Paterson, Lindsay 36
Pax Romana 62
performance maximisation 65
performance measures 30
performativity 7, 26, 30–1, 34, 40, 78, 91, 96, 104
permissive society 7, 13, 20–1, 26, 30, 32, 34, 40, 51, 91, 94–6
Peston, Robert 25
Pettifor, Ann 50
Philips, D.C. 90, 92
Piketty, Thomas 1, 76, 80
Plant, Sadie 40, 76
Plato 64, 88, 92, 95, 106
positive liberty 62
postmodern condition: postmodernism 40, 76, 78, 94, 101, 104
power 2, 6–8, 13, 15, 17–19, 22–3, 31–3, 37–40, 44, 46–51, 53–4, 59, 63–4, 66, 71–2, 76, 85, 87–9, 91, 95–6, 101, 104–6, 111
pragmatism 8, 16, 59, 77, 88, 94, 96, 102, 106
Pridham, Geoffrey 36
The Prince 31, 44–6, 50–3, 105
Professional Growth Plans 33
Program for International Student Assessment (PISA) 24
progressive education 7, 13, 20, 35–6, 38, 40, 51, 90, 92
progressivism 8, 30, 33, 35–8, 84
Protagoras 88
Public Choice theory 8, 16, 58
Puett, Michael 105–6

Queen Victoria 33

Race to the Top 33
Ramonet, Ignacio 78
Ramsden, Paul ix, 51
Rand, Ayn 3, 7, 13–22, 26, 34, 35, 38, 40, 48, 67, 94–5, 102, 105
rational choice 2, 8, 33, 58, 59, 61, 64, 67, 93
rationalist 8, 17, 18, 48, 58, 101–2, 103
rationality 7, 14–17, 19, 20–1, 25–6, 30, 31, 40, 48, 58, 66, 75
Reagan, US President Ronald 2, 32
Reformation 86
Registered Inspector 33

relate 24
Renaissance i, 1, 3, 5, 8, 31, 35, 44, 46, 52, 53, 86–8, 96, 105
Renaissance humanism 2–4, 6, 96, 105
Republican 93
Research Excellence Framework (REF) 79
rhetoric 3, 36, 87, 88
risk 7, 9, 13, 19–20, 22–5, 30, 34, 38, 39, 44, 52, 63, 75, 77, 80, 93, 95, 96, 103, 106
Robbins Report 91
Roe, John 45
Romantic 13–15, 17, 35
Rose, Jonathan 37
Rossiter, A.P. 13
Rothbard, Murray N. 19
Rousseau, Jean-Jacques 13, 36
Rubin, Dale 50
Ruskin Speech 38
Ryan, James 24, 51
Ryan, Kevin 93
Ryan, Kieran 5, 87

Sandel, Michael 1, 63, 64, 66
School Effectiveness Research (SER) 9, 78
School Improvements Grants (SIG) 78
School leader: school leadership i, 8, 44–5, 49–51, 53–4, 102–3
Schroeder, German Chancellor Gerhard 63
self-interest 8, 22–3, 31, 44–5, 59, 61, 64, 73–5, 79, 92–3, 96, 105
Seneca 69, 84, 86–7, 94
Shershow, Scott Cutler 74, 79
Siedentop, Larry 72
Sinfield, Alan 4
Situationist International 21
skills 9, 24–5, 60, 64, 76, 79, 84, 89, 91–3, 96, 102
Smith, Adam 3, 50, 58, 61, 63
Smith, Matthew 71
Smyth, John 1
social-constructivist theory 103
social evolution 17, 51, 54, 101–2, 104–5, 106
socialism 36, 48, 102
social justice 6, 8, 57, 76, 103
Socrates 106
solidarity 48, 75
Sophistry: Sophism 3, 88, 93, 94
Stoics: Stoicism 9, 71–3, 76, 84, 103
Stratford-upon-Avon 4, 85

Studia humanitatis 3
supernatural 15, 17, 46, 48, 53, 73, 102
surveillance 16, 31, 33, 40
Sutton Trust 77

Tadros, Victor 104
teachers 7, 13, 24, 30, 33–4, 38, 40, 44, 60, 76, 78–9, 84, 93, 104
Technical and Vocational Educational Initiative (TVEI) 91
Ten Laws for Students·36
terror 7, 21, 30, 31, 34, 40, 63, 76–8
Thatcher, Prime Minister Margaret 2, 13, 22, 32, 38, 92
theoretical contemplation 85–6, 89, 106
Third Way 63
Thomson, Leslie 73
Tillyard, Eustace 50
totalitarian: totalitarianism 2, 3, 7, 17, 21, 26, 30, 39, 44, 49–50, 52, 77, 95
tradition 2–3, 6–7, 14, 17–20, 36–40, 44, 49, 51, 70, 74, 89–94, 96, 101–2
truth claims 76, 80, 91, 93
Tuck, Eve 33

UK House of Commons Select Committee 24
unity 8, 36, 66, 73, 76, 101, 105
universe 52, 71, 72–5; abundant universe 79, 106
university 4, 14, 24, 60–1, 64, 91, 109
Uno solo 52
US Department of Education 77, 78
use-value 5, 70
utopia 9, 19, 26, 95–6, 106

Victorian England 36
von Gierke, Otto 31
von Goethe, Johann Wolfgang 14
von Hayek, Friedrich ix, 1–3, 6–8, 13, 16–18, 21–2, 34, 39, 44, 48–54, 58, 73–7, 92, 95, 101–4, 106
von Mises, Ludwig 19–20, 25

Way, The 105
Weber, Max 7, 18–20, 23, 25
'what works' 9, 76–9, 96, 104
What Works Clearinghouse (WWC) 77
Whitaker, Todd ix, 51–2
White Paper on Higher Education 60–1, 63–6
Wilde, Oscar 6
Wilkins, Andrew 75

Willetts, Minister for Universities and
  Science David 60–2
Williams, Joanna 91
William Tynedale Junior School 37
wisdom: 'the wise man' 3–4, 21, 45, 84,
  88–9, 94
Wissenschaft 36

Woods, Peter 33–4
World Bank 24

Young, Michael 37
Young Americans for Freedom (YAF) 21

Žižek, Slavoj 66–7